SUPRASEGMENTALS

SUPRASEGMENTALS

Ilse Lehiste

THE M.I.T. PRESS
Cambridge, Massachusetts, and London, England

P217
L37

FOREWORD

This book has grown out of an interest in suprasegmental phenomena that has largely determined the direction of my research for the last ten years. More directly, it is the outgrowth of seminars that I offered as guest professor at the University of Cologne in 1965 and at the Linguistic Institute held at UCLA in the summer of 1966. These seminars provided the impetus for organizing the accumulated material in the form in which it is presented in the book. In a way I have now written the book that I would have liked to have used as a textbook when I was teaching my seminars on suprasegmentals.

While I have attempted to survey all linguistically relevant evidence from the areas of production and perception, I have been constrained by the limits of practicality in the presentation of this evidence. The field of linguistic phonetics has important areas of overlap with many disciplines, including neurophysiology, anatomy, speech and hearing, psychology, and acoustics. It was obviously impossible to go into the kind of detail in each of these areas of overlap that would satisfy the specialists in these areas. The selection of material thus represents personal judgment of what is relevant for answering linguistically interesting questions.

I have not tried to work out a typology of suprasegmentals except to the extent implied by the chosen form of presentation. I have likewise not attempted to survey all languages of the world for examples of suprasegmentals. Much of the presented material derives from my own work, and thus the languages most frequently referred to are languages that I have investigated over a number of years: English, Estonian, Serbo-Croatian, Finnish, Czech, Latvian, Danish, Norwegian, Russian, German, and a few others. Looking back, I find that the study of suprasegmentals has in fact constituted the common factor that has been present in almost all my work: not knowing then that I would ever try to write this book, I seem to have been working on aspects of it all the time.

I would like to say a few words here explaining my attitude toward the phonetic evidence that I have taken some pains to assemble. For a linguist, phonetics is only a means toward an end, not a purpose in itself. The end is to provide reliable answers to linguistically relevant questions. However, for providing these answers, phonetics is indispensable. I believe firmly that true statements regarding phonological phenomena presuppose correct observation of their phonetic manifestation. A phonologist ignores phonetics at his own peril.

Much of the research on which this book is based was supported by the National Science Foundation grants G-18842 and GS-238. I am also grateful to Dr. Charles J. Fillmore of The Ohio State University, Dr. William S-Y. Wang of The University of California at Berkeley, and Dr. Peter B. Denes of the Bell Telephone Laboratories, who read the manuscript and made many constructive suggestions. I have incorporated as many of their suggestions as I could, and may indeed regret that I did not follow all of them. Last, but not least, I am indebted to Miss Marlene Deetz for her invaluable assistance with the manuscript.

Ilse Lehiste

Columbus, Ohio
January 1969

CONTENTS

SUPRASEGMENTALS

CHAPTER ONE
INTRODUCTION

The study of prosody is perhaps one of the oldest branches of the scientific study of language. Originally at home in classical philology, it acquired new importance in connection with the rise of comparative Indo-European linguistics in the nineteenth century. During the twentieth century, prosodic phenomena have become a part of linguistics that most linguistic schools have attempted to incorporate into the theory (see, for example, Jakobson, 1931; Trubetzkoy, 1939; Trager, 1941; Firth, 1948 [1957], who used the term in a somewhat different sense; Haugen, 1949; Pike, 1954, 1955, and 1960; Hill, 1961). Yet a certain degree of vagueness seems to characterize most discussions of prosodic features. They seem more elusive than segmental features, and their incorporation into a linguistic system sometimes seems to strain the limits of an otherwise coherent framework.

This vagueness extends to the definition of prosodic features. In American linguistics, the term is used more or less synonymously with suprasegmental features. Suprasegmental features are usually either listed as the set of features consisting of pitch, stress, and quantity, or defined as features whose domain extends over more than one segment (Hamp, 1957). A definition is preferable to a list; the definitions referred to, however, have at least two weaknesses. If suprasegmentals are to be defined with reference to their domain, then pitch, stress, and quantity would not qualify as suprasegmentals when they happen to be manifested over a single segment. On the other hand, if all features whose domain is larger than one segment are to be classed as suprasegmentals, then long components such as the voicing of a sequence of voiced segments would have to be included (Z. Harris, 1944), and the ranks of suprasegmentals would be swelled by such additional possible suprasegmental features as vowel harmony and pharyngealization. If it is true that stress, pitch, and quantity

1

behave in a way that sets them apart from features determining segmental phonetic quality, the definition should be revised.

I believe there is a difference in kind between segmental features proper and the features of pitch, stress, and quantity. The last three are, in a way, a secondary, overlaid function of inherent features. Voicing is an inherent feature that may be identified at a moment in time; pitch is an overlaid function of voicing. The fundamental frequency of a voiced segment may serve simultaneously to identify the segment as voiced and to constitute part of the manifestation of a tonal or intonational pattern. Every segment must have a certain duration in the time domain to be identifiable as a segment; the feature of quantity involves manipulation of inherent duration. Every segment, if it is to be realized phonetically, also has a certain amount of intensity (as a result of being produced with a given amount of articulatory effort); whatever the acoustic and physiological correlates of stress, they consist in intensifying phonetic factors already present in a lesser degree.

A further difference between segmental and suprasegmental features appears in the fact that suprasegmental features are established by a comparison of items in sequence (i.e., syntagmatic comparison), whereas segmental features can be defined without reference to the sequence of segments in which the segment appears, and their presence can be established either by inspection or paradigmatic comparison (i.e., comparison of an item with other items in the phonological inventory). For example, the rounding of a vowel in a sequence of rounded vowels can be established for each vowel without necessary reference to adjacent sounds. The stressedness of a vowel, on the other hand, cannot be established without comparing the vowel with another segment in the sequence. Thus the differences between suprasegmental features and segmental features are simultaneously differences of kind and differences in degree.

These characteristic differences between segmental and suprasegmental features make it possible to offer a tentative first definition of suprasegmentals: suprasegmental features are features whose arrangement in contrastive patterns in the time dimension is not restricted to single segments defined by their phonetic quality (i.e., distribution of energy in the frequency dimension). But the definition is hardly satisfactory, since it defines something in terms of what it is *not;* it does not bring us much closer to knowing what the suprasegmentals *are.*

The problem is further complicated by the fact that the same phonetic elements may also function on a paralinguistic level (Trager, 1958; Markel, 1965). Paralanguage has been delineated into two main areas: voice qualities and vocalizations. Voice qualities include such factors as pitch range, pitch control, resonance, articulation control, and tempo; vocalizations comprise, among others, such features as overloud and oversoft intensity, overhigh and overlow pitch, drawling and clipping, and pauses and other hesitation phenomena. Although paralanguage is not to be confused with language, it is found in systematic association with language. In a study of the suprasegmental function of pitch, stress, and quantity, their paralinguistic function has to be somehow accounted for.

Attempts have been made in the past to establish the phonetic correlates of prosodic features (Twaddell, 1953; Jakobson, Fant, and Halle, 1952). However, experimental phonetics has made great strides during recent years, and much new evidence has been brought to light that has an important bearing on the problem of suprasegmentals. In this book I intend to assemble and summarize what is currently known about the phonetic nature of suprasegmentals, and to evaluate the available evidence from the point of view of linguistic theory.

In order to have a linguistic function, a feature must be an independent variable; its realization cannot be conditioned by some other factor. In a study of the linguistic function of suprasegmentals, it is therefore necessary to start with the identification of all inherent constraints and conditioned variations. Only when all conditioning factors have been identified and eliminated may we consider the feature as an independently functioning constituent in the linguistic system of a language.

Table 1.1. Suprasegmentals

Suprasegmental	Physiological	Acoustic Manifestation	Perception	Phonetic Characteristics	Linguistic Function	
					Word Level	Sentence Level
Quantity features	2.1. Timing of articulatory sequences	2.2. Time dimension of the acoustic signal	2.3. Perception of duration	2.4.1. Intrinsic duration of vowels 2.4.2. Segmental conditioning 2.4.3. Intrinsic duration of consonants 2.4.4. Quantity and phonetic quality 2.4.5. Magnitude of relevant differences 2.4.6. Suprasegmental conditioning factors 2.4.7. Position within higher-level phonological unit as conditioning factor	2.5. Quantity	2.5. Tempo
Tonal features	3.1. Phonation	3.2. Fundamental frequency	3.3. Perception of pitch	3.4.1. Intrinsic pitch 3.4.2. Segmental conditioning 3.4.3. Dependence of tone upon phonation 3.4.4. Phonetic quality 3.4.5. Magnitude and kind of relevant differences 3.4.6. Suprasegmental conditioning factors	3.5. Tone	3.5. Intonation
Stress features	4.1. Physiological mechanism	4.2. Intensity and amplitude	4.3. Perception of loudness and perception of stress	4.4.1. Intrinsic intensity 4.4.2. Role of fundamental frequency, intensity, and duration 4.4.3. Suprasegmental correlates of stress 4.4.4. Segmental cues	4.5. Word stress	4.5. Sentence-level stress

I shall start, therefore, from a consideration of the physiological mechanism involved in the production of the phonetic phenomena under consideration, and I shall try to establish the physiological constraints within which the features may be manifested. The next stage will deal with the physical (acoustic) manifestation of this physiological process. I should like to make it clear, however, that the main emphasis in this book will be on production and perception; in the present context, the importance of acoustics lies in the fact that the acoustic signal is more easily available to study and measurement than neural events. The description of the acoustic correlates of the suprasegmentals will be followed by a consideration of their perception. Perceptual constraints are at least as important as the constraints involved in production; if an observed acoustic feature is to be considered distinctive, the obvious first requirement is that it be audible (i.e., above the perceptual threshold). I shall then attempt to identify the phonetic conditioning factors that may affect the manifestation of a suprasegmental feature. After all such conditioning factors have been identified and eliminated, I shall consider the linguistic functions of the feature at various levels—word level and sentence level.

Table 1.1 illustrates the scheme of presentation followed within the book. The references are to subtitles of Chapters 2, 3, and 4. An attempt is made in the fifth chapter to evaluate the findings presented in these three chapters from the point of view of their potential contribution to linguistic theory.

CHAPTER TWO
QUANTITY

This chapter is concerned with duration and its linguistic function. As was outlined in the introduction, it will deal first with the physiological mechanisms involved in producing quantity phenomena, then with their physical (acoustic) manifestation, with the perceptual correlates of quantity, with various phonetic phenomena connected with quantity, and finally, with the linguistic function of quantity.

2.1. Timing of articulatory sequences

The physiological mechanism that is ultimately responsible for quantity phenomena is the process involved in the timing of articulatory movements. In order for the feature of quantity to function significantly in language, it must be assumed that the timing of articulatory movements and their sequences can be controlled; in other words, that the duration of articulatory gestures and their ordering in sequence are not completely determined by physiological constraints such as the mechanical time constants of the motor structures.

Such physiological constraints exist nevertheless. It is necessary to identify them and to determine their scope, so that the extent of freedom may be ascertained within which the feature may function linguistically.

A considerable amount of work has been done in studying the speed with which articulatory movements are carried out. The average rates of articulation will be discussed under tempo (Section 2.5). At this point it might be useful to establish the upper limits of speed of which the articulatory organs are capable. The mechanical time constants may be inferred from these limits.

Some basic information was provided in a paper by Hudgins and Stetson (1937). In the research reported in this paper, the authors studied the maximum rate of articulation. Several subjects produced sequences consisting of three unstressed syllables followed by a stressed fourth syllable (*tat tat tat tat'*, *pu pu pu pup'*, *ka ka ka ka'*, *tun tun tun tun'*). The maximum rates of which the speakers were capable for the three unstressed syllables were determined. The number of movements per second for the tip of the tongue (*tat tat tat*) ranged from 7.2 to 9.6, with an average of 8.2; for the back of the tongue (*ka ka ka*), from 5.4 to 8.9, with an average of 7.1; for the lips (*pu pu pu*), from 5.7 to 7.7, with an average of 6.7; and for the velum (*tun tun tun*), from 5.2 to 7.8, with an average of 6.7. It becomes evident from these data that the tip of the tongue is the most mobile articulator; the larger the structures involved, the slower their response seems to be.

One might assume that these rates are completely determined by the size, mass, and shape of the articulators; the tip of the tongue being the smallest, its inertia is less than that of the other articulators. A single articulation of [t] is very similar to the individual closures produced with the tip of the tongue during the articulation of a trilled [r]. I performed a brief experiment in which I compared the rate of controlled tongue-tip articulation with the number of closures per second produced in the articulation of a sustained tongue-tip trill. I used an unaspirated alveolar [t] with an unrounded mid-central vowel, that is, sequences of the syllable [tə], produced at the highest rate of which I was capable. The syllables were repeated for an average of three seconds at a time, and [r] was sustained for an equal length of time. The mid-central vowel was selected because of its acoustic similarity to the vocalic portions of the tongue-tip trill (the vocoidal segments between the individual taps of the tongue). My results confirm Stetson's: I produced an average of 8 [tə] syllables per second. The rate of interruptions during [r] was considerably faster: I averaged 28 taps per second. The [r] sequences were also much more regular, and the duration of the individual taps more uniform, than was the case with the individual consonant articulations of the train of [tə] syllables.

This brief experiment suggests that the maximum rate of 8 syllables per second is not completely determined by the physical properties of the articulatory organ, in this case the tip of the tongue; if this were the case, the [r] oscillations would not be more than three times faster than the [t] articulations. It is more than likely that a large part of the rate of articulation depends on the speed with which neural commands can be translated into articulatory movements.

It is not presumed that each oscillation of the articulator (the tip of the tongue) in the production of [r] results chiefly from individual neural innervations of the articulator. These oscillations are viewed as an aerodynamic process involving a specified articulatory position and a balance of muscle tension, applied breath pressure, and airflow (Peterson and Shoup, 1966).

It is interesting that voluntary finger movements have an upper limit of the same magnitude—about 8 times a second—although a finger can be moved faster by electrical stimulation (Craik, 1948).

This suggests that the upper limit of a voluntary movement is determined by neurological constraints. It has been shown that the latency period of a simple motor reaction to a sound signal is of the order of 110 to 150 milliseconds; the time delay in responding to a proprioceptive signal is about 100 milliseconds (Kozhevnikov and Chistovich, 1965, and the literature quoted there; cf. van den Berg, 1962). Thus, the consonant articulations in rapid trains of CVCVCV syllables follow each other at intervals that seem to be very close to time periods determined by the response capability of the neural pathways.

It has been hypothesized that rapid sequences of movements, such as trains of CVCV articulations or the execution of complicated piano passages, consist of "ballistic" movements, i.e., that they have a predetermined time pattern and are "triggered off" as a whole (Craik, 1947; Lashley, 1951 [1961]). Ballistic movements, according to Craik, occur when a brief and predetermined force is exerted on a limb, which moves for a time, often greatly exceeding the duration of muscular contraction. Movements that fall into this category cannot themselves be modified, but if for one reason or another the intended goal is not reached, a secondary corrective movement may be employed. Speeds may be reached in such complex movements that rule out direct sensory control. One is led to postulate some central nervous mechanism that activates different muscles in predetermined order. This is particularly obvious in the case of ballistic movements, but the need for a correlating mechanism exists also in the case of individually controlled movements.

The problem of correlating the activities of different muscles so that articulatory events occur in the order intended by the speaker has been discussed in detail by Lenneberg (1967). The rate at which individual muscular events occur throughout the speech apparatus is of an order of magnitude of several hundred events every second. Lenneberg emphasizes that the activation of so many muscles in such a short time cannot depend on volition alone; there must be "preprogrammed" trains of events that run off automatically. These patterns are complex motor configurations that extend over periods whose duration may comprise that of a syllable or a word.

The existence of such patterns is further supported by anticipatory lapses in ordering: the well-known phenomena of metathesis and spoonerisms (Lashley, 1951 [1961]). Since such lapses involve the interchange of elements in sequences that have yet to be realized, their occurrence clearly implies the existence of a program for the realization of the sequences.

In summary, it appears highly likely that articulatory movements are indeed programmed as sequences. It seems, further, that the time patterns of these articulatory sequences are correlated with linguistic units, and that there exists a basic unit, of the size of a syllable, within which the time patterns are realized (Kozhevnikov and Chistovich, 1965).

2.2. *The time dimension of the acoustic signal*

The physical correlate of the timing of articulatory sequences is the time dimension of the acoustic signal. From a physical standpoint, speech constitutes variations in acoustic patterns as a function of time. The time dimension enters any description of speech—that of segmental sounds as well as their organization in the time domain. Since time is involved in the definition of frequency—periodic oscillations expressed as a function of time—the time dimension also enters the determination of phonetic quality, which is defined as the distribution of acoustic energy in the frequency domain. Strictly speaking, one cannot determine phonetic quality at a moment in time, since phonetic quality involves frequency, which presupposes time in its durative rather than momentary aspect.

However, when the suprasegmental feature of quantity is under consideration, the span over which the feature is manifested is potentially larger than a single segmental sound, and the time dimension of the acoustic signal functions simultaneously at several levels.

The physical duration of articulatory events is measurable with considerable precision. The problem is not so much in measuring as in determining the points at which to perform the measurements (Peterson and Lehiste, 1960). The investigator making the measurements faces the question of the meaningfulness of the results. It appears pointless to attempt greater precision in measurement than is warranted by the speaker's ability to control his articulatory apparatus, on the one hand, and the hearer's ability to discriminate among the durations, on the other. For example, if a vowel is articulated at a fundamental frequency of 100 Hz, and if its duration is presented in milliseconds, it seems to be implied that the speaker can control the articulation with a precision equal to having control over one tenth of one vocal fold vibration, which appears highly unlikely. Yet the time span between the closure and opening of a plosive articulation can be measured with comparable precision. A rough idea about the limits of sensory control over articulations was presented in the preceding section. The problem of the perception of duration is discussed in the following section.

2.3. The perception of duration

The perceptual correlate of the time dimension is the perception of duration. Summary treatments of the problem have been offered by Weber (1933), Woodrow (1951) and Wallace and Rabin (1960). Within the present context, two questions need to be answered: What are the minimal differences of duration that a human listener is capable of noticing, and should these differences be expressed as absolute values or as ratios? To give a concrete example, one might observe that two speech sounds have durations of 100 and 120 msec and wonder whether the difference might be linguistically significant. Before this can be determined, it is necessary to ascertain whether the difference of 20 msec is indeed audible, i.e., above the perceptual threshold. One might then encounter two sounds with durations of 200 and 220 msec. If the absolute differences in duration constitute the basis of perceived differences, the same difference should be perceived; however, if the differential threshold depends on a ratio, the difference between 100 and 120 msec might be perceptually equal to a difference between 200 and 240 msec.

The just-noticeable differences (JND's; also referred to as DL's, or difference limens) of duration have been subjected to extensive study over a long period of time. A considerable amount of work has been done in establishing the Weber ratios for various reference durations. The Weber ratio is the ratio $\Delta T/T$, that is, change in duration over reference duration. As is well known, Weber hypothesized that the ratio between the stimulus increment and the reference stimulus is a constant, and that these constant ratios apply to all sense modalities. Recent studies have shown that the Weber ratios for the perception of duration do not remain exactly constant (Henry, 1948; Small and Campbell, 1962; Milburn, 1963; Ruhm et al., 1966). There are certain differences between the several studies, which are probably partly due to differences in experimental method. Table 2.1 summarizes relevant information from three experiments in which the reference durations are within speech range.

The first column in Table 2.1 gives the reference durations, in milliseconds, used in the three studies. The next two columns report Weber ratios and mean absolute difference limens in

Table 2.1. Weber Ratios and Mean Absolute Difference Limens for the Perception of Durations Established in Three Studies (in msec)

	Stott, 1935		Henry, 1948		Ruhm et al., 1966	
T	$\Delta T/T$	Absolute DL	$\Delta T/T$	Absolute DL	$\Delta T/T$	Absolute DL
32			0.281	8.99		
40					0.0575	2.3
47			0.203	9.54		
60					0.0283	1.7
77			0.208	16.02		
80					0.0263	2.1
100					0.0260	2.6
110			0.196	21.56		
175			0.188	32.90		
200	0.142	28.4				
277			0.172	47.64		
400	0.120	48.0				
480			0.143	68.64		
600	0.115	69.0				

milliseconds, extrapolated from experiments performed by Stott (1935). Stott used a 1,000-Hz reference signal at an unreported sensation level (sensation level = intensity of the sound in dB above its absolute threshold level). The next two columns give mean Weber ratios (for seven subjects) and difference limens tested at seven reference durations by Henry (1948). Henry used a 500-Hz signal at 50 dB sensation level in this particular experiment. The last two columns give four Weber ratios and difference limens for ten subjects tested with a 1,000-Hz stimulus at 50 dB sensation level by Ruhm et al. (1966).

It is immediately apparent that the Weber ratios and difference limens established in the 1966 study are much smaller than those found in earlier studies. The research technique employed in the more recent study was probably more conducive to testing the limit of the auditory sensitivity of the subjects. It is quite likely that in a speech situation, where a great amount of external noise is present, the perception would not be as acute. It is perhaps a reasonable assumption that the difference limens established by Ruhm et al. represent the limit of perceptibility under optimal conditions, whereas it appears likely that in a speech condition, the just-noticeable differences established by Henry and Stott may apply.

In summary, it appears that in the range of the durations of speech sounds—usually from 30 to about 300 msec—the just-noticeable differences in duration are between 10 and 40 msec. This is important in judging the appropriateness of attempted accuracy of measurement. Some segmental boundaries can be established with considerable precision from acoustic records. Transitions between sounds with different manners of articulation usually involve a major change in the acoustic patterns. Transitions between sounds with the same manner of articulation, e.g., between two vowels, are much more difficult to determine. In general, boundaries are relatively easily established with reference to acoustic cues to the manner of articulation, whereas cues relating to the point of articulation are of practically no help. Obviously, the accuracy with which the beginning and ending of a segment are determined will have an effect on the measured duration. If the fluctuations that result from difficulty in establishing the boundaries are greater than the just-noticeable difference in duration, it is necessary to make the measurement technique more precise.

There are speech sounds that involve articulations whose durations are shorter than the shortest reference sound used in the three studies just reviewed, notably, the various flaps and taps and the single closures of a trill. Syllabic trilled [r] presents an interesting problem with respect to assigning acoustic (and articulatory) segments to phonemic entities: Are there some phonetic reasons that might determine whether a syllabic [r] should be analyzed as a uniform syllable nucleus or as a sequence of some vowel plus the consonant [r]? If the individual closures during [r] could be heard as separate events, this could be interpreted as evidence favoring the second analysis. I am not able to tell auditorily how many flaps are contained in a trill, although I can distinguish between a single tap and a multiple articulation. Analysis shows that in languages like Serbo-Croatian, a long syllabic [r] contains 4 to 7 individual closures; the vocoidal element before the first and after the last closure is no different in duration from the gaps between the closures.

There have been studies aimed at determining the accuracy with which subjects could count the number of short 1,000-Hz tones in a temporal series. Garner (1951) used rates of 4, 6, 8, 10, and 12 per second, with numbers from 1 to 20. He found that the accuracy of counting was a function of both number of tones and repetition rates. Very low numbers could be accurately counted at repetition rates as high as 12 per second, but at numbers above 5 or 6, counting accuracy decreased with rates of 6 or more per second. These rates are similar to syllabic rates, and considerably below the oscillation rates present in a tongue-tip trill (for this speaker, of the order of 28 closures per second).

Various experiments have been performed to determine the shortest time interval between two successive sounds that a human listener can actually hear as two. Rosenzweig and Rosenblith (1950) found that when the time interval between clicks presented to one ear was below 10 msec, a single click was heard that gradually became "double-humped" when the interval was increased. At 10 msec, the fusion ended and two separate clicks were heard. The value of 10 msec is close to the just-noticeable differences for the shortest speech sounds. However, with dichotic stimulation (i.e., with the signal presented to both ears), two clicks were heard as one when the interval between stimuli was less than 2 msec. When the interval was increased to 2 msec, fusion failed and the two clicks were heard as separate events.

In an earlier study, Wallach, Newman, and Rosenzweig (1949) had established that the interval over which fusion takes place for sounds in close succession varied with the kind of sound. A temporal interval of about 5 msec resulted in the fusion of single clicks, whereas the fusion interval between two more complex sounds was judged to be perhaps as long as 40 msec. This would account for the fact that individual closures cannot be auditorily distinguished during a syllabic [r].

Another interesting question is the minimum amount of time needed to decide which of two sounds occurred first—in other words, the role of just-noticeable differences in duration in the perception of temporal order.

In 1959, Hirsh published the results of a series of experiments designed to determine the size of the temporal interval between the onsets of a pair of sounds that enables the listener to determine which of the two elements came first. A separation time of between 15 and 20 msec was required for the listener to report correctly (75% of the time) the order in which the two sounds were presented.

Broadbent and Ladefoged (1959) found that failure to discriminate temporal order could occur over periods much longer than those found in Hirsh's study. Discrimination of order was at a chance level under some of their conditions, even though 150 msec separated their onsets ("buzz" relative to "hiss" and "pip" relative to "hiss"). After repeated exposure to the stimuli, the threshold fell to the order of magnitude found by Hirsh. Broadbent and Ladefoged suggest that their findings constitute evidence for a perceptual mechanism working on discrete samples of sensory information rather than on a continuous flow. When two stimuli fall in the same sample, their order is not immediately apparent perceptually; listeners have to be trained to interpret as order the cues that the ear transmits about the relative times of arrival of the stimuli. The authors conclude that their results give some indication of the minimum length of the perceptual sample, below which training is necessary before differences of order can be appreciated.

In both of these experiments, the investigators used non-speech stimuli. The relevance of psychophysical experiments in which clicks, pure tones, and noise are used as stimuli to the perception of speech is frequently questioned. In a recent study by Fay (1966), the test stimuli were extracted from sustained productions of /v/, /ð/, /z/, /r/, /ɾ/, /l/, /m/, and /n/. (The author is a speaker of general American, and /r/ was a retroflex continuant rather than a trill.) Various combinations of these were presented to listeners for the determination of the order of their presentation. The results indicated that temporal resolution varied considerably according to the speech sounds involved. Performance ranged from high accuracy at 10 msec onset disparities for m/r, n/r, v/l, and r/v, to failure to identify the order correctly even at 70 msec inter-onset disparity for m/n. Temporal resolution of a pure-tone pair, 1,200/250 Hz, was inferior to that found for one-half of the pairs involving speech sounds.

The just-noticeable differences in duration are also important in determining whether variations in duration produced by phonetic conditioning factors may possibly play a significant role. A number of phonetic conditioning factors are considered in Section 2.4.

A question that will arise in connection with phonetic conditioning factors may be anticipated at this point: To what extent is the perception of one suprasegmental feature influenced by other suprasegmental features? What is the role of frequency and intensity in the perception of duration?

Some psychoacoustic studies have dealt with the influence of either fundamental frequency, intensity, or stimulus quality (or a combination of them) on the perception of duration. Already, Henry (1948) had shown that discrimination was poorer for faint sounds. Wallach, Newman, and Rosenzweig (1949) showed that if two brief sounds are heard as fused into a single sound, the localization of the total sound is determined largely by the location of the first sound. This "precedence effect" in sound localization takes place when the two sounds are nearly equal in intensity. If the second sound is more intense than the first (more than 15 dB louder than the first sound), it overrides the precedence effect.

In the study referred to earlier, Hirsh (1959) found that the minimum time required for a correct judgment of temporal order between two sounds appeared to be independent of their difference in frequency when the sounds were of different pitch. The minimum time was the same when one of the sounds was a tone or click and the other a noise.

In a series of experiments, Creelman (1962) measured human ability to discriminate between durations of auditory signals presented in a noise background. Independent variables were the signal voltage, the base duration T, and the increment duration ΔT. Separate experiments assessed the effect of each of these on discrimination. Some of the results are relevant in the present context. When the increment was kept constant at 10 msec, detection fell off as base time was increased (in five steps) from 20 to 320 msec. When base time was kept constant at 160 msec and ΔT was increased, detection improved as a linear function of the increment duration. Detection of a duration difference (between 100 msec and 130 msec) increased rapidly with signal voltage, but only at low signal-to-noise ratios; the dependence became negligible when the signals were made "loud and clear" above the continuous background noise that was used in the experiment.

In the study by Small and Campbell (1962), test signals of 250 and 5,000 Hz were used, and no consistent frequency effect was observed. Ruhm et al. (1966), using frequencies of 250 and 1,000 Hz, likewise found that signal frequency had no effect on the magnitude of difference limens for duration. However, they discovered that sensation level affected the perception of differences in duration: a smaller limen was obtained at 50 dB sensation level than at 10 dB sensation level. Ruhm et al. also found that sensorineural hearing loss had no effect on the magnitude of the duration DL.

It thus seems that frequency has no effect on the perception of duration, whereas intensity increases up to a certain level tend to improve the listener's capacity for discrimination.

In trying to interpret the significance of these findings, one should keep in mind that it is far from known to what extent the results of psychophysical tests are applicable to speech perception.

2.4. Phonetic conditioning factors

2.4.1. Intrinsic duration of vowels The duration of speech sounds may be affected by several phonetic conditioning factors. To a certain extent, the duration of a segment may be determined by the nature of the segment itself, that is, by its point and manner of articulation. The term *intrinsic duration* may be used to refer to the duration of a segment as determined by its phonetic quality.

A great number of investigations have been devoted to problems of intrinsic duration. As far as the vowels are concerned, their duration appears to be correlated with tongue height: other factors being equal, a high vowel is shorter than a low vowel. This has been known for some time, and new observations provide additional confirmation. The languages in which this fact has been observed include English (Heffner, 1937; House and Fairbanks, 1953; Peterson and Lehiste, 1960; House, 1961), German (Maack, 1949), Danish (Fischer-Jørgensen, 1955), Swedish (Elert, 1964), Thai (Abramson, 1962), Lappish (Äimä, 1918), and Spanish (Navarro Tomás, 1916). Representative values might be quoted from Elert (1964), who measured long and short allophones of Swedish vowels before /t/ and /s/. Table 2.2 gives a short summary of Elert's findings. It may be noted that these differences are probably above the threshold for auditory discrimination and thus should be audible.

It is quite probable that the differences in vowel length

Table 2.2. Average Durations of Swedish Vowels (in msec)*

Vowels	Long Allophones		Short Allophones	
	No. of Occurrences	Mean Duration	No. of Occurrences	Mean Duration
/i y o/	89	140	126	95
/e u å/	141	155	107	103
/ä ö a/	126	164	133	111

* After Elert, 1964.

according to degree of opening are physiologically conditioned and thus constitute a phonetic universal. The greater length of low vowels is due to the greater extent of the articulatory movements involved in their production. Fischer-Jørgensen (1964a) advanced the hypothesis that the motor command for the timing is the same irrespective of the quality of the vowel, but that the execution of the command may be delayed owing to the movements to be made.

2.4.2. Segmental conditioning of vowel duration The influence of preceding and following consonants on the duration of a vowel has been studied with the same kind of thoroughness as the intrinsic duration of vowels. Much of this work has been done on the basis of acoustic analysis. Since acoustic phonetic techniques reached a relatively high level in English-speaking countries earlier than elsewhere, English has been most extensively studied, and there has been a slight tendency to assume that what holds for English is true in general. It so happens that in English, the voicing of a postvocalic consonant strongly affects the duration of a preceding vowel (House and Fairbanks, 1953; Zimmerman and Sapon, 1958; Peterson and Lehiste, 1960; House, 1961; Delattre, 1962a); unless this factor is taken into account, English is not a very suitable language for determining the influence of following consonants on preceding vowels.

One of the most carefully controlled studies of the influence of the place of articulation on duration was carried through by Fischer-Jørgensen (1964a). She used Danish nonsense syllables containing the vowels *i*, *u*, *y* followed by *b*, *d*, *g* (or *bə də gə*) and preceded by *h* or by the same consonant as that following the vowel. A second list of test words contained all possible consonants followed by −*udə* and −*idə*. The words were spoken by seven different subjects 6 or 12 times each; the test material contained 3,520 vowels, 2,106 postvocalic consonants, and 1,386 cases of "open interval" after initial stops. Fischer-Jørgensen established the differences in the durations of vowels in all environments, the durations of consonants, the differences between the durational relationships in monosyllabic and disyllabic words, and variations between speakers. The results of the study may be summarized as follows.

The duration of a vowel depends on the extent of the movement of the speech organs required in order to come from the vowel position to the position of the following consonant. The greater the extent of the movement, the longer the vowel. This explains the fact that all vowels were shorter before /b/ than before /d/ and /g/: since two different articulators are involved in the sequence vowel + labial, there is no time delay in moving the articulator (i.e., the tongue) from vowel target to consonant target. On the other hand, /u/ was particularly long before /d/. Before /g/, /u/ had an intermediate value; the movement involved is relatively small, but the back of the tongue is not as mobile as the tip of the tongue and the closing process takes more time.

Fischer-Jørgensen's findings agree with observations reported for English by Peterson and Lehiste (1960). In this study, short vowels were found to be longest before /t/, shorter before /k/, and shortest before /p/. For the voiced plosives, the order of the duration of short vowels was g > d > b (where the consonant letter means "vowel before the consonant" and > indicates "longer than"). The same order as for voiceless plosives was established for short vowels before fricatives and affricates: vowel length decreased in the order ʃ > s > f and z > v. Only for nasals was the order reversed: m > ŋ > n. For long vowels, the decreasing order before following consonants was t > k > p; d > g > b; ʃ > s > f; ʒ > z > v; and ŋ > n > m.

An increase in vowel duration, when the point of articulation of the postvocalic consonant shifts farther back in the mouth, has also been observed for Spanish. Zimmerman and Sapon (1958) listed average vowel durations before following consonants in Spanish disyllabic paroxytonic words as follows: [p] 93 msec, [β] 130 msec; [t] 104 msec, [ð] 136 msec; [k] 108 msec, [ɣ] 137 msec. (It cannot be concluded from these data whether the lengthening before the [βðɣ] set is due to voicing or frication.)

Some earlier studies had yielded different results. House and Fairbanks (1953) found that English vowels were generally longer before dentals than before labials or velars; however, in 1961 House found that the difference was negligible. Maack (1953) studied the problem in German. He found that front vowels were longer before labials and velars than before dentals; back vowels were longest before labials and shortest before velars. Maack formulated a rule for the influence of postvocalic consonants on the duration of vowels that is very similar to Fischer-Jørgensen's: The farther the point of articulation of a sonant from that of the following consonant, the longer the sonant. Maack also attempted to establish the influence of a preceding consonant on a following vowel. He stated that the sonant is proportionately longer, the closer its point of articulation is to that of the preceding consonant. This observation has not received confirmation from other studies.

The influence of preceding consonants on the duration of following vowels did not emerge clearly from Fischer-Jørgensen's study, partly because it was obscured by the different length of the open interval after the explosion. Since it is a matter of controversy whether the duration of the periods of frication and aspiration should be included in the duration of the vowel, it might be useful to review the matter briefly at this point.

The release of a plosive consonant usually involves two phases—explosion and frication—and may contain a third, aspiration. Fant (1958) has described the acoustic correlates of these phases as follows. The distinction between explosion and frication is a matter of source, explosion being the sound produced by the shock excitation of the vocal cavities due to the pressure release, and frication originating from turbulent sound produced by the following flow of air through the narrow passage that is formed immediately after the release. The duration of the explosion phase is limited by the decay time of the vocal cavities participating in the vibration. This time is the inverse of the bandwidth of the major resonance excited by the explosion; it is generally shorter than 15 msec. Fant accepts Fischer-Jørgensen's statement (1954) that aspiration is essentially an unvoiced version of the following vowel.

In the study reported in 1960, Peterson and Lehiste chose the center of the releasing spike as the point from which to begin the measurement of the duration of the vowel. Two separate measurements were made for syllable nuclei following aspirated plosives, the second one from the onset of voicing immediately after the aspiration. Peterson and Lehiste found that the duration of aspiration is conditioned by the point of articulation of the consonant. The average duration of the aspiration after an initial /p/ was 58 msec (for 81 different items); after an initial /t/ the aspiration lasted 69 msec (for 73 items); and for initial /k/ the duration of the aspiration was 75 msec (for 83 items). These data suggest that aspiration may become progressively longer as the point of articulation shifts farther back in the mouth, but this observation was not supported by a separate analysis of the two main allophones of /k/, [c] and [k]. The average for the front allophone, [c], followed by front vowels (39 instances), was 78 msec, whereas the average for the velar allophone [k], followed by back vowels (44 instances), was 72 msec. Nevertheless, the /t/ aspirations were consistently shorter than the aspirations associated with either of the allophones of /k/.

Fischer-Jørgensen (1964a) obtained similar results. She found that the duration of aspiration depends on two factors—the point of articulation of the consonant and the phonetic quality of the following vowel. For the sequence [pi], the duration of the aspiration was, on the average, 57 msec; for [ti], 74; and for [ki], 77. For the sequence [pu], the average duration of the aspiration was 66 msec; for [ku], 74. With both front and back vowels, the order of durations remained the same, but there were regular differences in the duration of the aspiration when the same consonant was followed by different vowels.

Fischer-Jørgensen also established the duration of what she

called "open intervals": the interval between the release of an initial consonant and the point at which the logarithmic intensity curve rises abruptly. The open interval corresponds to the period of frication defined above. Since the period of frication was included in the duration of the vowel by Peterson and Lehiste (1960) and by House (1961), and excluded by Fischer-Jørgensen, the results of vowel measurements in the two earlier studies are not completely comparable with those reported by Fischer-Jørgensen.

The durations of open intervals tended to fall between 20 and 30 msec. All seven speakers of Fischer-Jørgensen's study had a longer open interval after *g* than after *b* and *d*. Five speakers had a longer interval after *b* than after *d*, while two speakers showed the opposite relationship.

It is questionable whether the differences due to different duration of the open interval influence the perception of vowel duration in any real way, since they seem to fall within the difference limens established for the perception of duration.

It is interesting to consider whether the differences in the duration of frication (open interval) and aspiration are compensated for in the duration of the voiced part of the syllable nucleus. Evidence for this is not easily available, and much of it is unclear. In the Peterson-Lehiste study (1960), it was found that in 68 minimal pairs the average duration of the voiced part of the syllable nucleus after an aspirated voiceless plosive was 251 msec; when aspiration was included, the duration of the syllable nucleus was 308 msec; the average duration of syllable nuclei after voiced consonants was 274 msec. No obvious compensation can be deduced from these figures.

However, Kozhevnikov and Chistovich (1965) found that when a speaker repeats the same sentence many times, at the same rate of articulation, the durations of adjacent phonemes are quite strongly negatively correlated. Thus, if an error is made in the duration of one phoneme, the error is largely compensated for in the following phoneme. Chistovich argues from this that the timing of adjacent phonemes is not independent, but rather that the temporal sequence of articulation must be organized, at least in part, at levels higher than the phoneme.

Huggins (1968) ran a series of experiments to determine whether similar effects exist in perception. He measured just-noticeable differences for increases and decreases in the duration of a [p]-closure in a naturally produced sentence. The measurements were made on two versions of the sentence that were identical except for the duration of the stressed vowel that followed the [p]-closure. Changes in the duration of the [p]-closure itself had some interesting effects. The perceptual effect of a lengthened closure was that the speaker had hesitated in otherwise fluent speech. If the [p]-closure was greatly shortened, all subjects reported an apparent increase in speaking rate in the two unstressed syllables preceding the shortened closure. Huggins interprets this to mean that the whole temporal pattern of articulation was spontaneously restructured to assimilate the shortened closure. The restructuring extended from the prominence peak preceding the [p]-closure to the peak following it.

The influence of the manner of articulation of a consonant upon the duration of a preceding vowel seems to be largely dependent on the language. Even when nonsense words are used for test material, the linguistic background of the speakers shows through. This was the case with nonsense words spoken by the subjects of House and Fairbanks (1953); their results reflected the language-specific fact that in English, vowels are shortest before voiceless stops, and their duration increases, in this order, when the postvocalic consonants belong to the classes of voiceless fricatives, nasals, voiced stops, and voiced fricatives. Similar results were obtained with English test words in the study by Peterson and Lehiste (1960). Using minimal pairs and triplets such as *heat-heed* and *back-bag-bang*, Peterson and Lehiste established the durational ratio of vowel before voiceless consonant to vowel before voiced consonant as approximately 2:3. The influence of homorganic nasals differed but little from that of voiced stops; however, voiced fricatives had a further lengthening effect. In English, the differences are rather large and are clearly above the perceptual threshold. For example, the average duration of short vowels was 147 msec before /t/, 206 msec before /d/, 216 msec before /n/, 199 msec before /s/, and 262 msec before /z/.

Halle and Stevens (1967) have recently claimed that there are rather drastic adjustments in the positioning of the vocal folds and in the manner in which they vibrate when voicing is maintained during certain consonants. According to their argument, the wide separation of the vocal folds during voiceless consonants can be achieved more rapidly than the more finely adjusted smaller separation for a voiced consonant. This would explain the greater duration of vowels before voiced consonants than before voiceless ones. Halle and Stevens also report measurements of vowel duration in symmetrical CVC syllables in English, in which the consonants were /b/, /m/, /d/, and /n/. The values were as follows: for /b/, 270 msec; for /m/, 240 msec; for /d/, 310 msec; and for /n/, 260 msec. Data for each consonant represent averages over 36 utterances (12 vowels, 3 speakers). The authors suggest that the shorter duration of vowels before nasals than before homorganic voiced plosives is due to the special adjustment of the vocal folds which is needed to maintain vibrations during voiced plosives. No such adjustment is needed for voiced nasals.

The measurements presented by Halle and Stevens are at variance with the durations found during the Peterson and Lehiste study (1960), as well as with those reported by Elert (1964) for Swedish (to be discussed later). If, indeed, the manner of vibration of the vocal folds is different during the production of voiced plosives than during the production of voiced resonants such as nasals, the greater duration of a vowel before a voiced plosive should be a phonetic universal. The arguments of Stevens and Halle are effectively countered by Wang (1968b), who notes that the duration of an unchecked final vowel is comparable to that of a vowel followed by a voiced consonant; if the voiced consonant requires special adjustment of the vocal folds, which in turn takes more time than mere continuation of phonation, the vowels before voiced consonants should be regularly longer than unchecked vowels. Wang notes also that in sequences of vowel + glide, vowel + liquid, and vowel + nasal, the two members of the sequence shorten approximately proportionally before unvoiced consonants. If the durational difference were merely due to the adjustment time required by the following consonant, one might expect that the second member of such sequences would be influenced much more.

I am not aware of experiments performed to establish the perceptual significance of the relationship between vowel length and the voicing of the following consonant in languages other than English. However, experiments with synthetic speech (Denes, 1955) have shown that in English, vowel duration is an effective cue in the perception of voicing.

In trying to interpret the observed differences in vowel duration when followed by consonants produced with different manner of articulation, House (1961) proposed that the difference in vowel duration before stops and fricatives may be due to some inherent articulatory influences. He hypothesized that the articulation of stop consonants may represent less muscular adjustment from a physiological rest position of the vocal tract and may consequently require relatively less muscular effort than the production of sounds requiring more deviation from the rest position.

However, House observed that this kind of argument cannot be used to explain the influence of the voicing of a postvocalic consonant on the duration of the vowel. Voiceless consonants in English are typically described as fortis or aspirated; this characteristic suggests greater muscular effort during their production, when compared with voiced consonants. Nevertheless, English vowels preceding voiceless consonants are shorter in duration than those before voiced consonants. House concluded that the shortening of vowels before voiceless consonants is due to an articulatory activity arbitrarily imposed by the phonological system of English, and constitutes learned behavior in English rather than a phonetic universal.

For Swedish, Elert (1964) established much smaller differences in vowel duration due to the voicing of a postvocalic consonant. For example, short vowels followed by *t* were 13 msec shorter than short vowels followed by *d*. If a certain amount of increase before a voiced consonant is a universal feature, it is likely that its order of magnitude is closer to Elert's figures than to the large increases found in English.

Elert found also that short vowels followed by *t* were 14 msec shorter than short vowels followed by *s*. However, in Swedish, nasal consonants seemed to have a shortening influence on the preceding vowel: short vowels were 5 msec *longer* before *t* than before *n*, and 24 msec longer before *s* than before *n*. This suggests that either English or Swedish is deviant with respect to the effect of a following nasal on the duration of a preceding vowel. More research is obviously needed to establish the influence of postvocalic nasals on the duration of vowels.

In Spanish, a vowel is shortest before a voiceless plosive. If the duration of a vowel in that position is used as the basis of comparison (i.e., assigned the value 1), the vowels before voiceless fricatives have a duration of 1.13; before voiced fricatives, 1.27; and before /r/, 1.36 (Navarro Tomás, 1916).

The influence of the manner of articulation of a preceding consonant on a following vowel seems to be largely unexplored. More experiments, involving material from more languages, are needed to determine in which cases allophonic lengthening of vowels conditioned by phonetic environment is explicable in terms of the physiological process involved in the production of the sound, and when it is a language-specific feature learned by the speakers when they learn the language.

2.4.3. Intrinsic duration of consonants The intrinsic duration of consonants is influenced both by their point of articulation and by the manner of articulation. Most investigators agree that labials are longer than alveolars and velars, other factors being kept constant. Data for several languages show some disagreement about the relationship between alveolars and velars. Fischer-Jørgensen (1964a) found the following average durations (in msec) for the postvocalic /b d g/: in monosyllabic words, /b/ 101, /d/ 92, /g/ 94; in disyllabic words after short vowels, /b/ 71, /d/ 58, /g/ 57; in disyllabic words after long vowels, /b/ 72, /d/ 54, /g/ 60. Thus, /b/ always had a longer closure; the difference between /d/ and /g/ was not consistent.

Falc'hun (1951) found that in Breton, intervocalic /b/ had an average duration of 56.2 msec, /d/ 49.4, and /g/ 44.0; however, the order was different in the fortis (voiceless) series, in which the average duration of /t/ was 110 msec, /k/ 103.7, and /p/ 93.3. In initial position, the lenis /b d g/ had the average durations of 68, 56, and 52 msec, but the fortis consonants had a different order: /dd/ 95 msec, /bb/ 86 msec, and /gg/ 85 msec.

In a study of Estonian consonants (Lehiste, 1966), I found that short intervocalic /p/ had an average duration of 51 msec (in 16 instances), /t/ and /t'/ 30 msec (in 50 instances), and /k/ 36 msec (in 55 cases). The Breton data contradict the otherwise plausible assumption that dental/alveolar consonants should generally tend to be shorter than velars, since they are articulated with the most mobile articulator—the tip of the tongue. There is, however, a tendency in many languages to replace a dental/alveolar plosive with a tap or flap; consider the so-called voiced /t/ in American English (Sharf, 1962; Malécot and Lloyd, 1968), or the replacement of /d/ by single-tap /r/ in Finnish. Several of the shortest /t/'s were realized as flaps in the Estonian study. I have observed flapped dental/alveolar plosives in such diverse languages as Latvian and Tagalog.

Thus, there is some agreement concerning the labial point of articulation, whereas the relative order of the durations of dentals/alveolars and velars seems to vary either with position or with language.

To a certain extent, the duration of a consonant is also determined by its manner of articulation. It is obvious that a single flapped [t] articulation is shorter than a trilled [r], which involves a sequence of taps. It would seem that a fricative might be longer than a sound involving a closure; but this is not always the case. In the study referred to earlier, Falc'hun found that after a stressed vowel, the short (lenis) consonants had the following average durations: voiced plosives 56.5 msec, voiced fricatives 41.3 msec, nasals 51.7 msec. The comparable durations of long (fortis) consonants were: voiceless plosives 108.0 msec, voiceless fricatives 110.3 msec, nasals 96.1 msec. The durations of /l/ and /ll/ were comparable; /l/ 41.8 msec, /ll/ 90 msec. The duration of short /r/, 26.9 msec, indicates that it was realized as a single flap. The average of /rr/, 49.0 msec, suggests at least two closures during the trill.

Fintoft (1961) established the average durations of a number of Norwegian speech sounds. He found that unvoiced fricatives were always longer than any other consonants. There was a difference in the rank-ordering of other consonants, depending on the position of these consonants in the word. In initial and medial position, $s(f) > r > m(n) \geqq l > v$, whereas in final position, $s(f) > m(n) = v \geqq l > r$. (Here, $>$ means "longer than"; $\geqq$ means "longer than or equal to"; the parentheses indicate that /f/ and /s/, on the one hand, and /m/ and /n/, on the other, behaved in the same manner.) Some of the results here reflect specific Norwegian facts rather than universal phenomena.

Elert (1964) studied the duration of Swedish consonants in great detail. In a comparison of the plosives /p/ and /t/ with the fricatives /f/ and /s/, he found that the durations behaved differently when the test words occupied different places in the prosodic pattern of the sentence. In a list of isolated words, /p/ and /t/ had a significantly longer duration than the fricatives /f/ and /s/, but in a list of sentences, the unvoiced fricatives either showed no significant difference from the plosives or were longer.

In the study of Estonian referred to earlier (Lehiste, 1966), I found that intervocalic /s/ was always longer than a plosive.

In short phonemic quantity, the average duration of /s/ and /s'/ was 89 msec (for 53 occurrences); the averages for /p t t' k/ were 51, 30, and 36 msec, respectively.

It appears that except for taps, flaps, and trills, presently available information does not enable one to draw generally valid generalizations about the influence of the manner of articulation of a consonant on its duration.

2.4.4. Quantity and phonetic quality Certain problems arise in determining whether a length difference is distinctive when a difference in vowel length is accompanied by an equally noticeable quality difference. This happens in many languages (Straka, 1959). It is often true that a listener responds to either the quantity difference or the quality difference, disregarding the concomitant phonetic cues as allophonic. The native speaker's reaction may in such cases provide a suggestion as to which of the two—duration or phonetic quality—is of primary importance.

In most quantity languages that I have analyzed acoustically, I have observed some differences in the phonetic quality of long and short vowels. However, languages differ with respect to the extent and kind of influence the length of a vowel has on its quality. A comparison of Figures 2.1 and 2.2 illustrates the phenomenon.

Figure 2.1 presents an acoustical vowel diagram of short and long vowels in the first syllable of 571 disyllabic Czech words, produced by a native speaker. Figure 2.2 shows an acoustical vowel diagram of accented syllable nuclei occurring in 877 Serbo-Croatian words, likewise produced by one speaker. Since in the analyzed form of Standard Czech /l/, /r/, and /ou/ do not participate in the long-short opposition, they were not included in Figure 2.1. In Serbo-Croatian, syllabic /r/ occurs with all four accents, and the F_1–F_2 positions of the vocoidal parts of syllabic /r/ are presented in Figure 2.2.

The Czech vowel diagram shows that except for /ā/, long vowels have, as a rule, a smaller value for the first formant frequency, implying a higher tongue position. Long front vowels have a higher second formant than short front vowels;

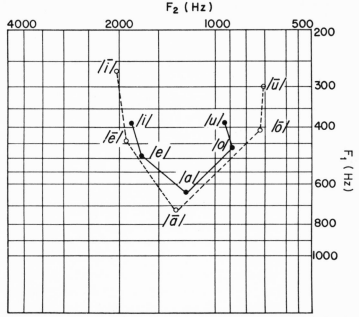

Figure 2.1. Acoustical vowel diagram of vowels occurring in the first syllable of 571 disyllabic Czech words produced by a native speaker. Filled dots represent average positions of short vowels; circles stand for average positions of long vowels.

the situation is reversed with the back vowels. In general, the acoustical vowel diagram suggests that the long vowels are characterized by more extreme values—positions farther removed from the center of the diagram.

The Serbo-Croatian diagram is more complicated, since the syllable nuclei differ in accent type as well as in length. It is nevertheless quite obvious that, first of all, accent type has no influence on vowel quality. It is also clear that /i/, /u/, and /r/ show no dependence on duration; /e/, /o/, and /a/, on the other hand, show a marked influence of quantity on vowel quality. Here the kind of influence is similar to that observed in Czech, but the extent of the influence is somewhat greater. The Serbo-Croatian pattern shows that short /i/ and /u/ need

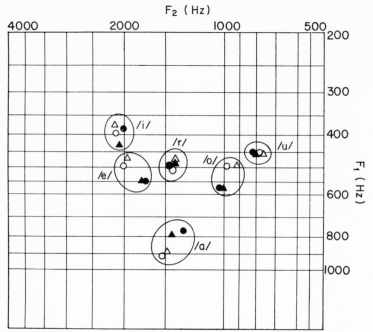

Figure 2.2. Acoustical vowel diagram of accented syllable nuclei occurring in 877 Serbo-Croatian words produced by one speaker. Filled dots represent syllable nuclei bearing the short falling accent; filled triangles represent average positions of vowels bearing the short rising accent; circles represent syllable nuclei with the long falling accent, and triangles stand for average positions of syllable nuclei with the long rising accent (reproduced from Lehiste and Ivić, 1963, p. 84).

not necessarily be centralized and lowered; thus, the centralization and lowering observed in Czech is not automatic. In Czech, the difference between long and short vowels is greatest for /i/ and /u/, whereas in Serbo-Croatian the greatest difference is observed in the mid vowels /e/ and /o/.

In English, vowels have both characteristic formant patterns and intrinsic durations that make it possible to group them into two sets according to length. The primacy of vowel quality over length in English has been the subject of some discussion (Delattre, 1962a). One factor that makes the primacy of vowel quality plausible in English is the extensive conditioning of vowel duration by the voicing of the following consonants, which counteracts intrinsic duration until the vowels of *bid* and *beat* may be equal in length. I have observed no comparable segmental conditioning of duration in languages with contrastive quantity.

Hadding-Koch and Abramson (1964) used an experimental approach to determine the relative importance of vowel quality and duration in Swedish. Using tape-cutting and tape-splicing techniques, they changed the durations of the stressed vowel and the postvocalic consonant in the word pairs *stöta/stötta*, *väg/vägg* and *ful/full*. Listening tests showed that length was the main cue for the pairs *väg/vägg* and *stöta/stötta*; however, for *ful/full*, which contains vowels differing considerably in phonetic quality, the experimental findings assigned little or no perceptual importance to relative duration.

It is interesting that in the original recordings of the test words, the short vowel/long vowel (V/V:) ratio for *väg/vägg* was 56% and for *stöta/stötta* 54%, whereas for *ful/full* the ratio was 80%. Elert (1964) found that in all types of material used in his investigation the ratio of the vowels occurring in this pair was higher than that of all other vowel pairs. Elert suggested that this might be due to a greater intrinsic duration of short /u/; Hadding-Koch and Abramson speculate that, whatever the historical situation in Swedish may have been, cue value shifted gradually from length to quality in this pair and as a result the constraint upon speakers to maintain a clear durational difference lessened.

It is not impossible that the present situation in English may have arisen through a similar process.

2.4.5. The magnitude of relevant differences The Swedish experiment brings into focus the following question: how large does a difference between long and short vowels have to be in order to be linguistically significant?

In languages in which stressed vowels have two contrastive

degrees of quantity, the V/V: ratio is close to 50%, but may vary a great deal. Data are available for a number of languages. In Danish (Fischer-Jørgensen, 1955) the average duration of short vowels was 50.5% of that of the long vowels. In a set of 1,440 disyllabic Finnish words, the ratio of short and long vowels of the first syllable was 44.1% (Wiik and Lehiste, 1968). In a set of disyllabic Estonian words (Liiv, 1962a), the average durations of the vowels of the first syllable were 118.8 msec for the first degree of length, 204.4 msec for the second degree, and 240.4 msec for the third degree of length; the ratio of short vowels to long vowels was 58.1%, short vowels to overlong vowels, 49.4%, and long to overlong vowels 85.0% (each average is based on about 300 measurements).

In a set of 877 Serbo-Croatian words (Lehiste and Ivić, 1963), the ratio of accented short vowels to accented long vowels was 67.2%. In Thai, Abramson (1962) found that the duration of long vowels (analyzed as geminates) was usually more than twice that of short vowels; in minimal pairs, the V/V: ratios were in the range of 28 to 50%. Abramson tested the relevance of duration as a cue experimentally, starting from geminate vowels and shortening them systematically. Listeners' responses showed a sudden increase in identification of the stimulus as a single vowel, when approximately 50% of the geminate vowels had been eliminated (cf. Bastian and Abramson, 1962).

In German, a considerable amount of work has been done by Zwirner and members of the phonometric school regarding the ratios between long and short vowels. Zwirner (1959, 1962) calculated ratios of V/V: for a number of German dialects and used them to establish isophones of quantity. The ratios range from 90.3% in the East to 51% in the West. The near equality in the duration of long and short vowels in some dialects raises the question whether in these dialects duration is the primary distinctive factor (Fourquet, 1964). The problem cannot be solved on the basis of description alone; experiments of the kind performed for Thai and

Swedish might provide decisive information. Until this kind of information is available for a large number of languages, it is impossible to state how large a ratio must be in order that duration may be considered distinctive.

A related question is how long must a sound be in order to be perceived as being present. Bastian, Eimas, and Liberman (1961) showed that inserting a sufficiently long temporal gap after the /s/-friction of the word *slit* induced the perception of /p/, giving the word *split*. In this experiment, the silent interval varied in 10-msec increments from 0 to 80 msec. The identification curves crossed the 50% line over a range of from 24 to 52 msec. The stimuli were presented for identification as *slit* or *split* and also for forced-choice discrimination. Discrimination turned out to be most acute in the region of the phoneme boundary, that is, the boundary between /p/ and its absence. Accuracy of discrimination, then, was determined almost entirely by whether the sounds in a given comparison were heard as different phonemes irrespective of the magnitude of the physical difference. Thus, the perception of this acoustic continuum was essentially categorical. Liberman et al. (1961, 1963) interpret these findings as evidence in favor of the motor theory of speech perception.

The suprasegmental features involve an articulatory as well as acoustic continuum; the articulatory reference hypothesis would lead one to expect a less precise partitioning in terms of phonemic identities, and hence little or no increase in acuity of discrimination at the boundary between phonemes. That this is indeed the case was shown by Bastian and Abramson (1962) in a cross-language study of the perception of duration by native speakers of Thai and English. Both groups were able to discriminate between stimuli differing in duration in an essentially continuous way with no evident effect of the phoneme boundary.

Besides providing additional evidence for the hypothesis that speech is perceived with reference to articulation, this experiment also supports the view that suprasegmental features can only be identified by comparison of items in sequence, and thus differ in a very essential way from features that may be identified by inspection of a segment (Jakobson, Fant, and Halle, 1952; Lehiste, 1967a).

2.4.6. Suprasegmental conditioning factors One of the problems in the study of suprasegmentals is their tendency to co-occur, so that it is difficult to decide which is the independent variable. In many languages, stress is one of the factors that conditions the duration of a sound or a sequence of sounds. Correspondingly, duration may be considered as one of the phonetic manifestations of stress. There are languages in which a stressed syllable is regularly longer than an unstressed syllable, other factors being kept constant. Among these languages is English. Parmenter and Treviño (1935) established that in English an average stressed vowel is approximately 50% longer than an average unstressed vowel. There are other languages in which stress seems to be manifested to a greater extent by other phonetic features, and increase in duration is minimal. Such languages include Czech, Finnish, and Estonian. Figure 2.3 illustrates the independence of quantity from stress in Czech. The figure shows the durations of syllable nuclei in the first and second syllables of 642 disyllabic test words in Czech, spoken by one informant. (The set includes the 571 words on which Figure 2.1 was based, as well as words containing the syllable nuclei /r/, /l/, and /ou/.) The number of occurrences is indicated on the vertical axis; the duration in centiseconds is shown on the horizontal axis. The first syllable is always stressed in Czech. The two sets of curves indicate that stress has no obvious influence on quantity.

An interesting phenomenon is the much greater scatter of values in long syllable nuclei compared to the short syllable nuclei. This would tend to support Trubetzkoy's notion that in a quantity opposition, the short member corresponds to a point in time, while the long member has a length dimension and is stretchable at will (*undehnbar* vs. *dehnungsfähig*; see Trubetzkoy, 1936, 1938).

It is perhaps necessary to separate word stress and sentence

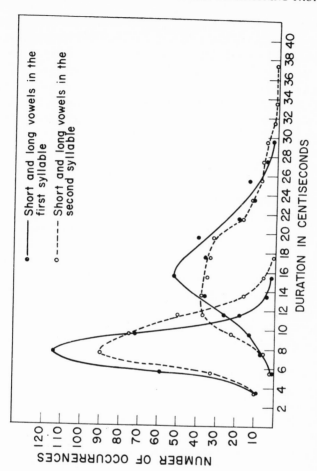

Figure 2.3. Duration of short and long vowels occurring in the two syllables of 642 disyllabic test words produced by one Czech speaker.

stress from emphatic stress in languages in which word stress has no appreciable influence on the duration of a segment or a syllable normally bearing word stress. The problem will be discussed further in Chapter 4.

In a language that has both length distinctions and tonal distinctions, one might expect a mutual interaction. In at least one language, Serbo-Croatian, it can be shown that this interaction need not take place (Lehiste and Ivić, 1963). In a set of 877 Serbo-Croatian test words produced by one informant, the average duration of stressed syllable nuclei bearing a short falling accent was 137 msec (for 271 items), that of vowels with short rising accent was 139 msec (for 269 items); the average duration of syllable nuclei with long falling accent was 210 msec (for 160 items) and that of syllable nuclei bearing a long rising accent was 199 msec (for 177 items). These differences are probably below the perceptual threshold.

Figure 2.4 (Lehiste and Ivić, 1963) presents graphically the duration of accented syllable nuclei in this set of words. The number of occurrences is indicated on the vertical axis; the duration in centiseconds is shown on the horizontal axis. The solid lines connect points representing the number of occurrences of syllable nuclei with indicated durations under falling accents; dotted lines connect corresponding points for syllable nuclei with rising accents. As may be seen from the figure, the durations of short syllable nuclei under both accents were quite similar and their range relatively small. A much lesser degree of concentration was observed in the case of the long accents; both curves, however, show a peak around 20 centiseconds. The scatter seems to be somewhat less than in the Czech case presented earlier (Figure 2.3).

Languages may also differ among themselves with respect to the manner in which speech tempo affects the duration of segmental sounds. In certain languages, an increase in speech tempo is largely achieved by shortening unstressed syllables, whereas in other languages, the decrease in duration might be proportional over the whole speeded-up utterance. English belongs among the languages of the first type, in which the

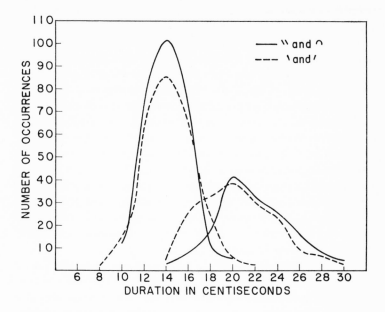

Figure 2.4. Duration of accented syllable nuclei in a set of 877 Serbo-Croatian test words.

duration of stressed syllables decreases at a much smaller rate than the duration of unstressed syllables.

This fact may be illustrated by a review of a brief experiment (Peterson and Lehiste, 1960). It is well known that in English there is a tendency for stress groups to assume approximately the same duration (Classe, 1939). If such isochronous groups include a varying number of syllables, their duration must vary according to the number of syllables included in the group; the spacing between main stresses tends to remain constant. We decided to keep the number of syllables constant in a series of frame utterances, and to vary the spacing between main stresses in a systematic way. To control the tempo, the subjects were asked to speak in synchronism with a periodic pulse produced over an earphone, so that the mono-syllabic test words bearing sentence stress coincided with the pulse. The speedup factors were computed from measurements made from acoustically processed tapes. In this experiment, the duration of syllables with main stress changed less than the duration of the unstressed syllables: when the rate of utterance was increased by a factor of two, the stressed words decreased in duration by a factor of approximately 1.5. Thus, the speedup was achieved largely at the expense of the unstressed syllables.

2.4.7. Position within a higher-level phonological unit as conditioning factor Another factor that influences the duration of a sound is its position within a higher-level phonological unit. This phenomenon is well known and has been observed in many languages (Malmberg, 1944; Jones, 1948). It appears that in some languages the word as a whole has a certain duration that tends to remain relatively constant, and if the word contains a greater number of segmental sounds, the duration of the segmental sounds decreases as their number in the word increases. An example may be drawn from a recent study of Hungarian (Tarnóczy, 1965). Table 2.3 shows the average duration, in milliseconds, of vowels in Hungarian words of from one to five syllables. These average durations show that the longer the word, the shorter the actual duration of the vowels, until a stressed phonemically long vowel in a relatively long word becomes comparable in duration to a

Table 2.3. Duration of Successive Vowels in Hungarian Words (in msec)*

Word	1st Long	2nd Short	3rd Short	4th Long	5th Short
[ta:t]	210				
[ta:tog]	180	145			
[ta:togɒt]	140	95	115		
[ta:togɒto:k]	120	85	105	130	
[ta:togɒto:knɒk]	110	80	90	110	140

* After Tarnóczy, 1965.

phonemically short unstressed vowel in a shorter word. Since the duration still remains contrastive (i.e., does not change from phonemically long to phonemically short), it must be concluded that the listener interprets the duration of a particular sound by relating it to the duration of the word as a whole.

In certain other languages, unstressed syllables may be regularly longer than some stressed syllables. In Estonian, the duration of a vowel in an unstressed second syllable is, as a rule, longer than that of a vowel in a stressed short first syllable. Thus, the phonetic duration of the vowel of the second syllable is conditioned by its occurrence in that syllable: the conditioning factor consists of the position of the sound within a higher-level phonological unit. The quantity system of Estonian will be discussed in greater detail further along in this chapter.

All the factors summarized on the preceding pages influence the duration of phonological units. In considering conditioned variation, one should not overlook another source of variation: differences between various productions of the same utterance by the same speaker and by different speakers. Under otherwise identical conditions, a speaker produces durations that are normally distributed within a range characteristic of the speaker. These variations are likewise without linguistic significance and must be discounted. Differences between speakers are often quite large. The problems involved in interpreting the observed scatter have been discussed in detail by Zwirner and Zwirner (1936 [1966]); phonometric methods have been critically evaluated by Fischer-Jørgensen (1964b). The relevance of statistical methods in phonetic studies is also discussed by Fischer-Jørgensen (1959) and Elert (1964), among others.

2.5. Duration as an independent variable at word level and sentence level

Any variation in duration that can be shown to be conditioned, either by the nature of the segment itself or by external conditioning factors, cannot function significantly at the same time as part of the system of oppositions employed in the phonology of the language. Assuming that all conditioned variation has been identified and accounted for, one may consider further durational features found in a language as independent variables. The term *quantity* will be applied to duration when it functions as an independent variable in the phonological system of a language.

2.5.1. The domain of quantity One problem that arises in considering the function of quantity in a language is the determination of its domain. There are languages in which short and long sounds are opposed to each other; the domain of quantity in these languages would seem to be a segment. (The possible analyses of segmental quantity will be discussed later.) In such languages, the occurrence of length on a segment is not conditioned or restricted by surrounding segments, although there may be some word-level restrictions; in Finnish, for example, initial and final consonants do not participate in the opposition.

There are other languages in which the quantity of a given segment must be related to the quantity of other segments in the sequence. For example, in Icelandic, Norwegian, and Swedish (Elert, 1964) there exists an inverse relationship between the quantity of a vowel and that of the following consonant, so that a short vowel is followed by a long consonant, and a long vowel by a short consonant. The domain of the placement of quantity patterns here appears to be a syllable.

In still other languages, quantity patterns have domains that are larger than a single syllable. In Slovak, the unit that is taken into consideration in the assignment of quantity is a disyllabic sequence, since in this language two long syllables may not follow each other (Trubetzkoy, 1939 [1962]).

In Estonian, and probably in a number of other languages, the domain of the quantity patterns is the word; there is some evidence that words are in turn built up of certain disyllabic sequences (Lehiste, 1965b; cf. also Chapter 5).

2.5.2. Linguistic analysis of quantity There are several ways in which quantity may be analyzed linguistically. Quantity manifested over a single segment may be analyzed as a prosodic distinctive feature. This has been the practice within generative phonology (Harms, 1968). Long vowels and consonants then would have [+long] included in their list of distinctive features. This would seem to be especially appropriate for some languages in which quantity oppositions are restricted to a small subset of speech sounds. In Spanish, for example, the quantity opposition is limited to the pair /r/ and /rr/ (*pero* 'but'-*perro* 'dog'); the language knows no further quantity oppositions, neither in consonants nor in vowels. Here length appears indeed to function as a qualitative characteristic of the segment symbolized as /rr/.

Languages as diverse as Lebanese Arabic (Nasr, 1960) and the Kalenjin languages (Tucker, 1964) have been analyzed as possessing segmental quantity.

Another way to handle the fact that there are long and short sounds in a language is to list long and short vowels and/or consonants in the phonemic inventory of the language. This doubles the number of units in the inventory, and if indeed the system is symmetrical, it would be more economical to extract length from the system and treat it as a prosodeme (Haugen, 1949). Daniel Jones (1948) proposes the term *chroneme* to denote a set of lengths that count as if they were one and the same.

In many languages it is appropriate to treat long sounds as clusters of two identical sounds (Hockett, 1955; Swadesh, 1937). There are many ways in which the appropriateness of this analysis can be shown. In Latin, for example, the placement of stress depended on the quantity of the penultimate syllable: if the penultimate syllable was long (i.e., contained a long vowel or a short vowel + consonant), the syllable received word stress, but if it contained a short vowel, stress was shifted to the antepenultimate syllable. A simpler formulation of the rule would state that word stress was always placed on the penultimate mora relative to the last syllable. A long vowel thus functioned as if it contained two time units (morae), equivalent to two short vowels or to the sequence of a short vowel + consonant. The analysis of long sounds as sequences of two morae is discussed extensively by Trubetzkoy (1939 [1962]).

The treatment of long vowels as clusters of identical segments is especially appropriate if the language contains diphthongs, and if the long vowels and diphthongs occupy similar positions within the phonology. This is the case in Slovak (Trubetzkoy, 1939 [1962]) and Finnish.

With long consonants a further complicating factor enters the discussion: the possible phonetic realization of long consonants as geminates. The question of whether there is any phonetic difference between long consonants and geminates has been debated for some time; a survey of the different views was provided by Hegedüs (1959). Stetson (1951) presented experimental evidence that the so-called double intervocalic consonants do, in fact, involve two distinct maxima in the curves indicating the movement of the lips (for labials) or of the tongue (for linguals). The curve of the air pressure in the mouth likewise showed two peaks. Hegedüs (1959) studied long consonants in Hungarian and found no evidence for their geminate nature. My own preliminary studies of intervocalic /p/ and /pp/ in Estonian show two clear maxima in electromyographic recordings of the activity of the orbicularis oris muscle.

If a language has consonant clusters that function in the same manner as long consonants, it may be useful to analyze these long consonants as clusters of identical consonants regardless of whether it is possible to demonstrate, phonetically, their geminate nature. For example, Finnish short and long consonants contrast in every position except word-initial and word-final; in native Finnish words, no clusters occur in these positions either. Thus, even if the phonetic geminate status of the long consonants were uncertain, they could be treated as clusters because of this analogy.

There is, however, good reason to assume that in Finnish

the intervocalic long consonants have, at least at an earlier stage of the language, been true geminates and have contained a syllable boundary. The evidence for this is primarily historical (Itkonen, 1946). In describing the development of the alternation of the so-called strong and weak degrees in disyllabic stems in Lappish and Finnish, Itkonen notes that the behavior of the postvocalic consonant at the boundary of the first and second syllables differs in principle from that observed at the boundary of the second and third syllables. The consonant between the first and second syllables is subject to alternation, while the consonant between the second and third syllables provides the conditioning factor. If there is a single consonant between the second and third syllables, the stem consonants appear in the strong degree; a cluster of two consonants or a long consonant between the second and third syllables causes the appearance of the weak degree. The weak degree appears also in disyllabic words ending in a consonant. Itkonen concludes that the conditioning factor is really the placement of the syllable boundary, which falls before a single intervocalic consonant, but between the two members of a cluster or a long (geminate) consonant. Since final syllables are closed by a single consonant, an opposition between short and long consonants (i.e., single and geminate consonants) can be relevant only in intervocalic position.

In other languages—such as Estonian and Hungarian—oppositions between long and short consonants can, nevertheless, be found in word-final position. Contrasts in initial position are reported for Celtic languages (Falc'hun, 1951). In such cases an analysis of long consonants as geminate clusters has less compelling force.

The treatment of long sounds as clusters of two identical sounds presupposes a two-way quantity opposition. There are languages in which more than two contrastive durations have been observed. Among these is Estonian. In *The Principles of the International Phonetic Association* (1949 [1961]), a sample transcription of Estonian is given in which overlong sounds are written with three phonetic symbols.

This transcription implies an analysis of overlong sounds as clusters of three identical sounds. The question of whether Estonian has two or three distinctive quantities has been debated for decades (Ariste, 1938; Trubetzkoy, 1939 [1962]; Durand, 1946; Posti, 1950; Jones, 1950; Raun, 1954; Must, 1959; Lehiste, 1960b; Harms, 1962; Liiv, 1962b; Tauli, 1966; Lehiste, 1966; Hint, 1966). Those who question the relevance of three degrees of quantity admit the existence of a three-way opposition but propose to interpret the so-called overlength as a combinatory variant of length; the feature differentiating the overlong from the long degree is sometimes treated as tone (Durand, 1939), sometimes treated as "postposed stress" (Harms, 1962). There is some recent evidence (Lehiste, 1967b) that for vocalic syllable nuclei the domain of the feature of overlength is the syllable rather than a segment (or one of a sequence of segments). In this recent study, I found that overlong diphthongs differ from long diphthongs by a proportional increase in the duration of both components of the diphthong. This supports the analysis of overlength as a feature of the syllable. However, in a sequence involving a short vowel followed by an overlong consonant, the overlength does not extend to the vowel preceding the overlong consonant.

Some representative durations of vowels in the first syllable of disyllabic Estonian words are given in Table 2.4. The table also illustrates several phenomena discussed earlier in this chapter. The high vowels /i ü u/ ([i y u]) have a shorter intrinsic duration than the mid vowels /e ö õ o/ ([e ø ə o]) and the low vowels /ä/ and /a/ ([a ɑ]). The ratio between short and long vowels is 58.1%. As was mentioned earlier, the unstressed vowel of the second syllable is longer than a stressed short vowel (the relationship between the quantities of the vowels of the two syllables will be discussed more thoroughly in Chapter 5).

The difference in the durations of overlong and long vowels is less than the difference between long and short vowels. This may be partly due to the presence of other phonetic features in the case of overlong vowels. Regardless of whether

Table 2.4. Average Durations of Vowels in Disyllabic Estonian Words (in msec)*

Vowel	Words in quantity 1			Words in quantity 2			Words in quantity 3		
	No.	V_1	V_2	No.	V_1	V_2	No.	V_1	V_2
/i/	33–38	107.4	170.0	30–35	182.1	122.4	30–35	233.6	98.4
/ü/	33–38	105.0	136.7	30–35	177.7	116.6	30–35	218.6	98.5
/u/	33–38	104.8	173.9	30–35	195.9	130.2	30–35	241.3	102.4
/e/	33–38	116.9	160.2	30–35	214.9	131.6	30–35	232.6	81.2
/ö/	33–38	127.6	163.2	30–35	205.9	123.5	30–35	242.4	87.3
/õ/	33–38	130.9	159.2	30–35	196.7	133.7	30–35	242.9	98.1
/o/	33–38	125.1	155.8	30–35	225.0	135.3	30–35	259.9	84.5
/ä/	33–38	124.5	167.3	30–35	218.6	117.4	30–35	245.7	93.0
/a/	33–38	122.5	208.0	30–35	223.5	134.0	30–35	245.9	94.6
Total/ Average	313	118.8	162.9	283	204.4	127.1	284	240.4	93.1

* After Liiv, 1962.
V_1 = vowel of first syllable; V_2 = vowel of second syllable.

these features may be considered primary or allophonic, over-length has a durational component. As was mentioned earlier, this extra duration is distributed over both members of an overlong diphthong.

Phonetic descriptions of Lappish (Lagercrantz, 1927; Itkonen, 1946) suggest the existence of more than three degrees of quantity in that language. Unfortunately, it does not become clear from the presented phonetic data to what extent these phonetic durations may be considered distinctive (Ravila, 1962).

Three-way quantity oppositions have been further proposed for Hopi (Whorf, 1946) and Mixe (Hoogshagen, 1959). Trubetzkoy (1939 [1962]), who had learned about Hopi from Whorf before the publication of Whorf's materials, reanalyzed the three-quantity system of Hopi as consisting of two privative oppositions whose unmarked member is the vowel of medium length.

To my knowledge, no instrumental data are available for either Hopi or Mixe. The description of Mixe offered by Hoogshagen suggests that vowel quantity in Mixe is segmental, i.e., does not depend on syllable structure or on word patterns as was the case in Estonian. At least two minimal monosyllabic triplets are reported, in which the three vocalic quantities occur in identical environments. Three-way contrasts are found for each of the six vowels of the language. Possibility of con-ditioning by a preceding or following consonant is excluded by the fact that the same vowel appears in all three lengths while following or preceding the same consonant; the third length cannot be interpreted as containing another syllable, since every syllable must begin with one or more consonants. The three-way opposition is realized in stressed syllables (as demon-strated by the monosyllabic words); the long versus extra-long vowels have not been found to contrast in unstressed syllables.

Hoogshagen analyzes the third mora of overlong vowels as an allophone of /h/, on the basis of complementary distribution and phonetic similarity: the language has syllable nuclei of the type short vowel + h, but lacks syllable nuclei consisting of long vowel + h. Thus a phonetic [v:] is represented as /V·h/.

"Overlength" has also been claimed to exist in standard German (von Essen, 1957). In a recent study, Hanhardt et al. (1965) showed that no systematic distinction between pairs such as *wider* and *wieder* could be found.

It has been proposed (Trubetzkoy, 1939 [1962]) that what has been called quantity in many languages is really a difference in contact between the vowel and the following consonant ("Silbenschnittkorrelation"). Fliflet (1962) has shown that the term *contact* is misleading. Fliflet recorded test words in languages in which an opposition between "close contact" and "loose contact" is supposed to exist. He shortened long vowels by cutting off part of their beginning. Although the transitions from the vowels to the consonants had been left intact, listeners reported that what had formerly been "loose contact" now made the auditory impression of "close contact." Shortening of a consonant (by cutting off part of its middle and again leaving the transitions untouched) had the effect of changing a perceptual "close contact" to "loose contact." It appears that the listeners react to certain kinds of cues associated with syllable structure and the placement of a syllable boundary. It is the interaction of the durations of the vowel and the postvocalic consonant that determines the overall impression.

It was suggested earlier that in some languages the domain of quantity patterns is the syllable. Among these are the modern Nordic languages (Icelandic, Norwegian, and Swedish). Several analyses are possible in these languages; all of them have been considered by Benediktsson (1963). The point at issue is the well-known mutual complementation of vocalic and consonantal quantity: a short vowel is followed by a long consonant, and a long vowel by a short consonant. One possibility would be to consider quantity significant wherever it appears; thus, the phonemic inventory would contain long and short vowels as well as long and short consonants. Two additional possibilities would assign the distinctive function to either the vowels or the consonants and treat the length of the other set as dependent. A fourth possibility, adopted by Haugen (1958), makes quantity part of the "accent," together with stress (and, to some extent, pitch) and assigns it to the syllable as a whole. Benediktsson adopts the solution according to which quantity is relevant in the consonants, while vocalic quantity is automatic. The criteria that he applied in arriving at this solution need not have similar relative weight under other conditions; the situation prevailing in the language under analysis determines the preferable solution in each individual case.

As an example of a quantity system in which the domain of quantity patterns is larger than a single syllable, I would like to refer again to the quantity system in Estonian. The problem has received considerable attention within the last fifty years, and this is not the place for detailed comments on various theories; I have treated these problems extensively elsewhere (Lehiste, 1960b, 1965b, 1966, 1968a; for views differing from mine, cf. Posti, 1950; Harms, 1962).

Vowel length is contrastive in the first syllable of a word; but the phonetic realization of the (noncontrastive) duration of the vowels in nonfirst syllables is strictly conditioned by the order number of the syllable in which the vowel appears, and by the quantity of the preceding syllable. Syllables may have three quantities. Short syllables contain a short vowel, which is followed by a short intervocalic consonant. Long syllables may contain either a long vowel followed by a short consonant, or a short vowel followed by a long consonant, or a long vowel followed by a long consonant; in the latter two instances, the syllable boundary falls within the consonant. An overlong syllable contains at least one overlong sound—vowel, consonant, or both.

Now the duration of the vowel of the second syllable, which is not independently contrastive, is inversely proportional to the quantity of the first syllable (see Table 2.4). This is especially clear in case of short first syllables, which are followed by unstressed syllables whose vowel is usually about $1\frac{1}{2}$ times as long as the short vowel of the stressed short syllable.

This so-called half-long vowel may occur in other syllables than the second in longer words when it follows a contrastively short syllable (whose contrastive quantity is determined by the consonant, as discussed later). For example, in a word of four syllables in which all vowels and consonants are phonemically short (whenever an opposition is possible), the vowel of the first syllable will be contrastively short, the vowel of the third syllable noncontrastively short, and the vowels of the second and fourth syllable half-long. Representative vowel durations in such four-syllable words, averaged from 14 occurrences, are 79 msec for the first vowel, 105 for the second, 59 for the third, and 96 for the fourth (Lehiste, 1968a).

Vowel quantity is not contrastive in nonfirst syllables, but consonants may appear in contrastive durations between any subsequent vowels. The number of possible oppositions is either two or three, depending on the order number of the syllable. Three contrasts are possible in the duration of plosive consonants between odd and even syllables—between the first and second, third and fourth, fifth and sixth, etc. Three contrasts occur likewise between even and odd syllables if the preceding odd syllable is overlong. Only two contrasts occur between even and odd syllables if the preceding odd syllable is short or long but not overlong. Phonetically, the duration of the long consonant in positions where only two contrasts occur is intermediate between the durations of consonants in the long and overlong degree that occur in positions where a three-way contrast may occur.

It is clear that the phonetic realization of vowel length and particularly consonant length depends on the position of the segments within the sequence of syllables. The domain of the quantity patterns in this language is a higher-level phonological unit, which may be called a phonological word; in fact, a phonological word could be defined (for Estonian) as the stretch over which the quantity patterns are manifested.

2.5.3. *Tempo* The function of quantity on the sentence level is quite different from its function at the word level. Changes of the relative durations of linguistic units within a sentence do not change the meanings of individual words; however, they do convey something about the mood of the speaker or about the circumstances under which the utterance was made.

A considerable amount of information exists regarding the average rates of speech which may be considered "neutral" or unmarked. Significant changes from the unmarked rates constitute use of the feature of quantity at sentence level, manifested as changes in tempo.

In a series of studies, Goldman-Eisler has established the average rates of speech and some of the factors that condition them (Goldman-Eisler, 1954, 1956, 1961, 1967; Henderson, Goldman-Eisler, and Skarbek, 1966). Goldman-Eisler found that the speed of the actual articulation movements producing speech sounds occupied a very small range of variation—4.4 to 5.9 syllables per second (1961). The range of pause time in relation to speech time was five times that of the rate of articulation. Factors influencing the rate of speech included differences in cognitive processes such as selection, abstraction, or planning in speech, as well as emotional attitudes.

Whether there are differences in the rates of speech of speakers with different linguistic backgrounds is not well known. Goldman-Eisler's studies deal with syllabic rates. The speech rate of Hungarian speakers has been analyzed in terms of phoneme production (Fónagy and Magdics, 1960). Fónagy and Magdics found that the speed of utterance differed according to the circumstances of speech production. In reading poems, their subjects uttered an average of 9.4 sounds per second; in sports broadcasts, the rate reached 13.83 sounds per second. The average speed was 11.35 sounds per second. The difference in the phonological structures of Hungarian and English is such that the results of Fónagy and Magdics are hardly comparable with those of Goldman-Eisler.

Osser and Peng (1964) compared the rate of phoneme production in the speech of some American English and Japanese subjects and found no significant difference between the rates in the two groups.

2.5.4. Summary The duration of sounds may be conditioned by the following factors: point and manner of articulation of the segment itself; preceding and following segmental sounds; suprasegmental factors (especially by stress); and position of the sound within a higher-level phonological unit.

Duration may function as an independent variable at word level (quantity) and sentence level (tempo). The domain of quantity patterns may be a single segment or a higher-level phonological unit—a syllable, a disyllabic sequence, or a word. The possible analyses of quantity include treatment of quantity as a segmental distinctive feature; analysis of long sounds as clusters of short sounds or as sequences of two (or more) morae; inclusion of short and long sounds as separate entities in the phonemic inventory; and extraction of quantity as a prosodeme of length.

CHAPTER THREE
TONAL FEATURES

The suprasegmental feature considered in this chapter is commonly referred to by such terms as pitch, tone, and intonation. In this chapter, some of the terms will be restricted in their use: *pitch* will be used to refer to the perceptual correlate of frequency, *tone* will be used to refer to the feature when it functions distinctively at word level, and *intonation* when the feature functions at sentence level. The general term *tonal features* will be used to refer to all aspects of the linguistic use of fundamental frequency and its physical and perceptual correlates.

3.1. *Physiological correlates of tonal features*

The physiological correlate of the features of tone and intonation is the vibration of the vocal folds in phonation. The anatomy and physiology of the larynx have been studied in detail for some time, and descriptions of the larynx are found in phonetics handbooks (e.g., Gray and Wise, 1959, Chapter 3). The various theories of phonation have recently been reviewed by Lieberman (1967). I propose to give a brief outline of the myoelastic-aerodynamic theory of phonation, primarily following van den Berg (1958).

The vocal folds are approximated through the activity of the laryngeal muscles. A high-velocity airflow is created through the activity of the respiratory musculature. Passing through the constriction in the larynx, the airflow creates a pressure drop across the glottis; the negative pressure calls forth the so-called Bernoulli effect; as a result, the vocal folds are drawn together (van den Berg, Zantema, and Doornenbal, 1957). When the glottis (i.e., the opening between the vocal folds) is closed, the Bernoulli force ceases. The controlled tension of the musculature of the vocal folds tends to restore the vocal folds to their neutral position; the continued subglottal pressure forces them apart again, and the cycle repeats itself over and over again. The rate of the vibration depends on a number of interdependent factors: (1) the mass of the vibrating part of the vocal folds; (2) the tension in the vibrating part of the vocal folds; (3) the area of the glottis during the cycle, which determines the effective resistance of the glottis and the value of the Bernoulli effect in the glottis; (4) the value of the subglottal pressure; and (5) the damping of the vocal folds.

The first factor has been studied thoroughly by Hollien and Curtis (1960) and Hollien (1962). The results of these studies indicate, first of all, that individuals with low fundamental frequency levels exhibit larger, more massive vocal folds than do individuals with higher fundamental frequency levels. As the fundamental frequency increases, the mean thickness of the vocal folds is systematically reduced. The same observation was made for vocal fold cross-sectional area.

In another paper, Hollien (1960b) reported results of measurements of the length of vocal folds under different conditions. He showed that as the fundamental frequency of phonation is raised, the vocal folds systematically lengthen.

The tension of the vocal folds during phonation at different fundamental frequencies was studied experimentally by van den Berg (1962), who used excised human vocal ligaments, which were loaded with various weights. Longitudinal tension in the ligaments, expressed in grams per square millimeter cross-section, could be precisely controlled with this technique. Van den Berg showed that maximum elongation and tension resulted in high frequency of vibration.

Activity of the intrinsic laryngeal muscles during phonation was also studied by electromyographic techniques by Faaborg-Andersen (1957). His results indicate that during phonation, electrical activity in the adductor muscles increases markedly. When the increase in discharge frequency of a single motor unit during phonation could be determined, the resting frequency in cricothyroid and vocal muscles was found to be up to about 12 per second and to increase before the onset of phonation to 15 to 30 per second. This frequency was maintained during phonation; at the cessation of phonation, the frequency fell rapidly to 12 per second or less.

With rising fundamental frequency there was an increase in electrical activity in all the adductor muscles while electrical activity in the abductor muscles was inhibited. No significant increase in electrical activity occurred in the intrinsic laryngeal muscles with increasing intensity of phonation.

The air resistance of the larynx and the Bernoulli effect on the glottis were measured by van den Berg, Zantema, and Doornenbal (1957) by experiments on a cast of a normal fresh human larynx. Static volume velocities up to 2 liters per second and/or subglottal pressures up to 64 cm water were used in the experiments. Some of the results are as follows. The bulk of the air escapes under conditions of turbulent flow, whatever the form of the larynx may be, and the flow is then proportional to the area of the glottis and to the square root of the subglottal pressure. The pressure at the outlet of the glottis is negative because of the sucking Bernoulli effect and amounts to about half the value calculated on the assumption that energy losses are negligible; the mean pressure in the glottis effectively contributes to the stiffness of the vocal folds.

As the pressure and flow increase, the rate of vibration of the vocal folds also increases, both because the increased flow produces an increased Bernoulli effect so that the vocal folds are drawn together more quickly and because the increased pressure causes the vocal folds to be blown apart after a shorter closed phase.

Both van den Berg (1957) and Ladefoged (1967) have demonstrated that fundamental frequency increases when subglottal pressure is suddenly increased (by having a blindfolded subject phonate at a constant frequency and pushing him in the stomach at unpredictable moments). Ladefoged observes that the considerable changes (of the order of 10 to 40 Hz) in fundamental frequency must be due to the subglottal changes rather than to a reflex action affecting the tension of the vocal folds, since there is no delay between the subglottal pressure changes and the fundamental frequency changes; in all known human reflexes the response occurs at least 100 msec after the stimulus.

Finally, fundamental frequency of the larynx depends on its coupling to the rest of the vocal organs—the lungs and the trachea on the one hand, and the vocal cavities on the other (van den Berg, 1958). Problems arise when the impedance of the trachea and lungs or vocal cavities approaches the impedance of the generator, that is, when the fundamental frequency approaches a resonant frequency of either trachea and lungs or vocal cavities, as the impedances are then of the same order of magnitude. When the formant is somewhat higher than the frequency of the vocal fold vibration, the fundamental frequency is lowered; when the formant is somewhat lower, fundamental frequency is raised. Even with the fundamental tone approaching a formant, the difficulty in maintaining phonation is usually small, since the larynx can decrease excessive supraglottal pressures by increasing the damping of the formant by means of increased energy losses toward the vocal cavities or, respectively, the trachea and lungs. This increase is brought about by a slight change of the vibratory pattern, the mean area of the glottis during the cycle becoming slightly larger.

The fundamental frequency is also lowered when the resistance of the vocal cavities is suddenly increased without compensation in the larynx. The lowering of the fundamental frequency during the individual closures of a trilled [r] provides an example. This already was shown to happen during the production of [r] in Finnish by Pipping (1899).

The coupling with the subglottal system introduces a resonant frequency (that of the trachea and connected bronchi) at approximately 300 Hz. When the fundamental frequency approaches this frequency, the larynx may slightly change its vibratory pattern to increase the damping of the subglottal system. Lieberman (1967) noted that his subjects tended to avoid phonation at fundamental frequencies that would excite the 300-Hz subglottal resonance.

The limits within which the rates of vibration may change are partly determined by the size and mass of the vocal folds. Hollien (1960a, and in other quoted papers) has shown that laryngeal size is significantly smaller in speakers with high-pitched voices. There is also a very high negative correlation between the cross-sectional measures of the vocal folds and the absolute fundamental frequency of phonation. For any given speaker, the cross-sectional area and especially the mean thickness of the vocal folds are systematically reduced with increases in the fundamental frequency of phonation.

There are obviously limits beyond which the vocal folds cannot be tensed any further. The vocal ligaments can be stretched about 20 to 40% of their rest length through the application of relatively large forces (van den Berg, 1962), on the order of 300 grams per square millimeter. The passive longitudinal tension that the ligaments can bear is much larger than the active longitudinal tension that skeletal muscles, such as the vocalic muscles, can produce. A mean figure for maximum active skeletal muscle tension is 50 grams per square millimeter cross-section. The physiological factor of the finite size of the vocal folds in humans helps determine both the lowest and the highest rate of phonation of which a speaker is capable.

The difference in the size of the vocal folds is partly responsible for the difference in the ranges of men, women, and children. Typical median fundamental frequency levels are from 134 to 146 Hz for men, and 199 to 295 Hz for women (Cowan, 1936). Fairbanks (1940) showed that for adult males reading factual material, the fundamental frequency usually falls within the one octave frequency range 80 to 160 Hz. The average fundamental frequencies of 33 men, 28 women, and 15 children who served as speakers in a study by Peterson and Barney (1952) were 132, 223, and 264 Hz.

The larynx is capable not only of different rates of vibration but also of different modes of vibration. Catford (1964) describes more than ten states of the vocal folds that may be linguistically significant. At least one of these (in addition to the regular mode of phonation) appears to have suprasegmental function. It is the type called "creak" by Catford, who describes the physiological process involved as a low-frequency periodic vibration of a small section of the vocal folds. Catford assumes that only a very small section of the ligamental glottis, near the thyroid end, is involved, and that the mean rates of airflow are very small. The vibrations have a frequency of about 40 cycles per second, and the mean rates of flow are of the order of 12.5 to 20 cm³ per second. For comparison, Catford suggests that for normal chest voice at about 100 Hz the liminal rate of flow is about 50 cm³ per second, maximal about 230 cm³ per second. My own measurements of rates of airflow in phonated and whispered speech (Lehiste, 1964b) yielded an average of 503 cm³ per second for vowels produced with normal phonation by four men and three women.

The same phenomenon has been studied, under the name "vocal fry," by Hollien et al. (1966) and Hollien and Wendahl (1968). These authors define vocal fry as a phonational register of frequencies lying below the frequencies of the modal system. They measured a large number of samples of intentionally produced "vocal fry," finding that most of them involved repetition rates below any level that might be expected for a normal mode of phonation. The ranges were from approximately 28 to 73 pulses per second. One of the samples involved biphasic phonation, which had been previously described by Timcke, von Leden, and Moore (1959). In that study, ultraslow motion pictures revealed that as the "fry" was produced, the vocal folds vibrated in a biphasic pattern: each vibratory cycle consisted of a rapid sequence of two movements, followed by a prolonged period of approximation. The transition from normal phonation to biphasic phonation did not change the number of individual pulses per second, but did change their arrangement. When a sound that had a frequency of approximately 150 Hz changed to "fry," the length of the complete (biphasic) vibratory cycle corresponded to a frequency of 75 Hz, and a "subharmonic" appeared at this frequency, which was audible in conjunction with the primary tone at 150 Hz. The two movements differed in amplitude: the amplitude of the first excursion of the biphasic cycle was 20 to 25% smaller than the amplitude of the second excursion. While evidence for this doubling activity is available from acoustical sources, the more common pattern present in laryngealization appears to be one of a single pulse followed by a period of no excitation. Another characteristic of vocal fry is nearly complete damping of the vocal tract between successive excitations.

Timcke, von Leden, and Moore (1959) also showed that a voice quality subjectively labeled as harshness or hoarseness was associated with irregular vibrations of the vocal folds and the presence of aperiodicity in the signal.

When these modes of vibration are used in a linguistically significant way, I prefer to use the term *laryngealization*, referring to irregular, biphasic, or unusually slow vibration of the vocal folds.

3.2. Fundamental frequency

The acoustic correlate of vocal fold vibration is the fundamental frequency of the sound wave generated at the glottis. The acoustic structure of sound waves has been the subject of intensive study over a number of years. Reports of original research, handbooks, and introductory treatments of the physics of sound and the acoustic structure of speech are easily available (Joos, 1948; Fant, 1960; Ladefoged, 1962a; Ungeheuer, 1962; Flanagan, 1965); therefore, I shall confine myself to the barest outline.

It is customary to consider the sound wave that results from the successive openings and closings of the glottis as a periodic wave. Strictly speaking, only waves with an infinite number of exact repetitions of the cycle are periodic; the treatment of speech sound waves as if they were periodic is somewhat arbitrary, although convenient. There is evidence (Lieberman, 1961; Husson, 1960) that normal phonation in speech is considerably less than regular. Lieberman noted that in 86% of cases studied, the period duration was not steady over a three-period sample. The magnitude of the difference between the durations of adjacent periods was greater than 0.6 msec 20% of the time, and greater than 1 msec 15% of the time. Husson compared phonation during speech with phonation during singing, and found much greater regularity in the latter, although the rate of vocal fold vibration (expressed as number of cycles per unit time) was the same in both cases.

The relative aperiodicity of sound waves produced at the glottis seems to contribute to the naturalness of speech; it is quite probable that part of the unnaturalness of many samples of synthesized speech may be due to the excessive regularity of the fundamental frequency generator (Holmes, 1963).

For practical purposes, however, speech waves may be considered periodic. As periodic waves they share certain properties of all periodic, single-valued functions: they can be represented as the sum of a number of sinusoidal waves whose frequencies are integral multiples of the fundamental frequency, differing among themselves in amplitude and phase. These individual sinusoidal components are called harmonics; the term used in music is overtone (with the complication that the fundamental frequency is simultaneously the first harmonic, whereas the counting of overtones begins with the first harmonic above the fundamental, so that "first overtone" is another name for the *second* harmonic). The statement regarding the analysis of complex waves into sinusoidal components was formulated by Joseph Fourier, a nineteenth-century French mathematician; harmonic analysis is frequently called Fourier analysis.

We are at the moment concerned with one of the basic properties of a sound wave, namely, its *frequency*. Frequency is the number of complete cycles that take place in a given unit of time (a second). The time taken to complete one cycle is called a *period*. A simple relationship exists between the frequency of a vibration and its period: frequency (F) is the reciprocal of the period (T):

$$F = \frac{1}{T}$$

Thus, a sound with a frequency of 1,000 cycles per second (Hz) has a period of 1:1,000 second, or one millisecond; a period of 5 msec corresponds to a fundamental frequency of 1:0.005 = 200 Hz.

The rate of opening and closing of the vocal folds is directly reflected in the fundamental frequency of the sound wave produced at the glottis.

Various acoustic analysis methods exist for determining the fundamental frequency of the sound wave. My own experience with spectrography and with various fundamental frequency analyzers (Ivić and Lehiste, 1965) indicates that it is relatively more difficult to achieve desired precision in the measurement of fundamental frequency than in the measurement of duration. In order to decide what precision should be attempted in the analysis of fundamental frequency, it is necessary to consider the differential threshold for the perception of pitch.

3.3. The perception of pitch

Considerable attention has been devoted in the literature to the frequency characteristics of tonal stimuli and to their perception (Shower and Biddulph, 1931; Boring, 1940; Harris, 1952; Rosenblith and Stevens, 1953; Flanagan and Saslow, 1958). Differential sensitivity for frequency has been shown to depend upon a number of factors. Rosenblith and Stevens (1953) found that two methods of testing the same subjects yielded significantly different results: the difference limens (DL's) established by the AX procedure were less than one-half of the difference limens for the ABX procedure. Observers may also differ a great deal in sensitivity. Table 3.1 illustrates the differences between two subjects and two procedures. Rosenblith and Stevens also found that the size of the difference limen was influenced by such factors as practice, ensemble of stimulus conditions, and difficulty of the test. The authors doubt the wisdom of postulating a "true" difference limen, since it depends so greatly on a given set of conditions.

The data in Table 3.1 might be compared with median difference limens for three subjects, as reported by Harris (1952) (Table 3.2). Harris showed that the absolute DL uniformly decreases with frequency. Sensitivity improved

Table 3.1. DL's in Frequency for Two Subjects, Measured by Two Procedures*

Frequency (Hz)	Sensation level (dB)	Subject I			Subject II		
		DL/AX (Hz)	DL/ABX (Hz)	DL ABX / DL AX	DL/AX (Hz)	DL/ABX (Hz)	DL ABX / DL AX
250	30	0.34	0.72	2.1	1.4	5.4	3.1
1,000	30	1.2	2.5	2.1	3.5	8.9	2.5
1,000	60	0.9	1.9	2.1	2.9	8.9	3.0
4,000	30	8.7	1.6	1.8	23.0	94.0	4.1

* After Rosenblith and Stevens, 1953, p. 982.

Table 3.2.   Median Difference Limens
for Three Subjects*

Frequency in Hz	Median DL in Hz
125	0.74
250	1.33
500	2.09
1,000	3.61
2,000	8.28
4,000	21.09

* After Harris, 1952, p. 754.

with increasing loudness level; the effect of loudness level was slight for the lower tones but profound for the higher tones. When the frequency effect, as such, was eliminated by using the Weber ratio ($\Delta f/f$) as the index of sensitivity, it appeared that the relation of sensitivity to loudness level was constant over a wide frequency range.

Flanagan (1957b) published a summary statement concerning estimates of the maximum precision necessary in quantizing certain dimensions of vowel sounds. Summarizing his earlier studies, Flanagan suggested that the DL for fundamental frequency is of the order of ± 0.5 to $\pm 1.0\%$ for a vowel having a fundamental frequency in the neighborhood of 120 Hz. In a later study employing synthetic vowels and the fundamental frequencies of 80 and 120 Hz, Flanagan and Saslow (1958) found that the just discriminable changes in fundamental frequency were of the order of 0.3 to 0.5 Hz, and were, in general, slightly less than the frequency changes discriminable in a pure tone of the same frequency and sound pressure level. Thus, it should be necessary to quantize fundamental vocal frequency in steps of about ± 1 Hz in the octave range 80 to 160 Hz, which is the range usually employed by adult male speakers (Fairbanks, 1940). Attempted accuracy of measurement should likewise be of the order of ± 1 Hz in the fundamental frequency range.

The fact that the absolute differential threshold varies with frequency raises the question of whether a listener responds to absolute (linear) differences in frequency or to ratios between frequencies. There is abundant evidence that pitch perception is not linear. The difference between 200 and 100 Hz is perceptually different from the difference between 300 and 200 Hz, although the absolute difference is 100 Hz in both cases. On the other hand, the difference between 400 and 200 Hz is in an important way perceptually the same as that between 200 and 100 Hz.

There is a connection between musical intervals and the harmonics of a periodic complex sound. The simplest, most consonant musical intervals are those formed between the fundamental frequency and the successive harmonics. The ratio between the second and the first harmonic is $\frac{2}{1}$; the interval is an octave, and it is perceptually the same, regardless of the frequency of the fundamental. The ratio between the third and the second harmonic is $\frac{3}{2}$, corresponding to a pure fifth. A drop from 450 Hz to 300 Hz constitutes an interval that is perceptually equivalent to any drop involving the same ratio: 600 to 400 Hz or 240 to 160 Hz. The perceptual equivalence of intervals involving the same ratio makes it possible, in the analysis of tone languages, to discount the differences in vocal range that are so apparent between individual speakers.

Subjective pitch thus increases less and less rapidly as the stimulus frequency is increased linearly, and more and more rapidly as the stimulus frequency is increased logarithmically. (The musical scale is a logarithmic scale.) Stevens and Volkmann (1940) established the mel scale, which relates perceived pitch to frequency. The pitch of a 1,000-cycle tone, 40 dB above the threshold, is defined as 1,000 mels.

Several other facts about pitch perception have some intrinsic interest, although they are less important in the study of the linguistic function of fundamental frequency. One of these is the range of audible frequencies. The lowest rate of vibration to produce the impression of identifiable pitch is approximately 16 Hz; the upper limit is approximately 20,000 Hz (Fletcher, 1934). The absolute threshold (i.e., the intensity at which a sound is just discriminable from silence) for low-frequency tones remains essentially constant for most listeners throughout the span of life, but the thresholds for high-frequency tones increase markedly for advancing age. Roughly speaking, the loss of sensitivity at frequencies above 4,000 Hz amounts to 10 dB for each decade after 30 years of age (Licklider, 1951).

Most of the experiments concerning pitch perception have been performed using pure tones as stimuli. The sound produced by the vibrating vocal folds is a complex sound, rich in harmonics. There is evidence that the subjective pitch of a periodic complex sound depends on the periodicity of the waveform, regardless of whether there is energy present at the frequency of the fundamental or not. Schouten (1940) presented a complex tone to a group of listeners that contained components at 300, 500, 700, 900 cycles, and so on. The listeners equated the pitch of this tone with that of a 100-Hz pure tone. Schouten reports that a complex wave consisting entirely of frequency components above 3,000 Hz is heard as having a pitch of 200 Hz if its components are spaced along the frequency scale at multiples of 200 cycles.

The suggestion that pitch depends essentially on periodicity rather than on the presence of pure tones or harmonic structure of the sound wave receives some support from observations reported by Miller and Taylor (1948). Miller and Taylor studied the perception of repeated bursts of white noise, which they turned on and off at different rates. When the rate of interruption was between 40 and 200 per second, listeners were able to match the interrupted noise in pitch to a pure tone with reasonable accuracy. In this case, pitch appears to depend solely upon fluctuations in the rms pressure of the sound wave (rms = the square root of the mean of the squares of the instantaneous sound pressures; Licklider, 1951). The pitch of voiced fricatives is probably due to an analogous phenomenon: noise produced at the point of constriction is intensity-modulated by the periodic airflow variations (Fant, 1958).

The dependence of pitch upon loudness was studied by Snow (1936). Using several frequencies between 75 and 1,000 Hz and loudness levels within the range of 20 to 120, Snow found that all consistent judgments gave pitch shifts downward with increasing loudness, but there were large differences between individuals. Two of the nine observers perceived no shifts at any frequency or loudness, while three others experienced changes greater than 35% at the highest intensity. The frequency of greatest shift increased from about 100 Hz at small loudness to about 200 Hz at loudness level 120.

A similar experiment involving duration was carried out by Doughty and Garner (1948), who studied the perception of pitch level as a function of duration. They found that the pitch of a tone remains relatively constant down to durations of 25 msec, being affected seriously only at durations considerably shorter. As the duration of tones is decreased, there is a tendency for all tones to lose pitch, i.e., to be equated in pitch with tones of lower fundamental frequency that are sounded for a longer time. The amount of pitch loss is related to intensity and frequency. Pitch loss is greatest for high intensities and is somewhat less for lower intensities. Low frequencies show the greatest amount of pitch loss; high frequencies at low intensities show actual pitch gain for short durations. Within the speech range (at 250 Hz), pitch loss was 1 to 2% at an intensity of 70 dB and a duration of 12 msec; at 6 msec the pitch loss was 4%.

The duration of one period of a 250 Hz signal is 4 msec. It thus appears that more than three cycles of the wave were needed to give the listeners a firm feeling of perceived pitch. This is true in general for frequencies below 1,000 Hz: two or three cycles of the wave must be heard for the sound to have any predominant pitch at all (Licklider, 1951). Above 1,000 Hz a fixed length of time—about 10 msec—is required for the perception of pitch, rather than a fixed number of cycles. Somewhat shorter durations make the auditory impression of a click with discernible tonal quality; durations of 2 to 3 msec produce only a click with no subjective pitch attribute.

3.4. *Phonetic conditioning factors*

3.4.1. Intrinsic pitch There is a connection between vowel quality and the relative height of the average fundamental frequency associated with it: other factors being kept constant, higher vowels have higher fundamental frequency. Observations to that effect have been made for American English by Peterson and Barney (1952) and House and Fairbanks (1953). In a study published in 1961, Lehiste and Peterson reported the results of a detailed analysis of an intonation contour. A total of 1,613 sentences were analyzed in the study. The utterances consisted of a frame sentence in which test words were embedded; the peak of the intonation contour occurred on the test word. Fundamental frequencies were measured at the peak of the intonation contour and were averaged for each syllable nucleus. The results are summarized in Table 3.3.

Figure 3.1 presents the same data graphically. The lower curve represents values obtained in the study by Peterson and

Table 3.3. Average Fundamental Frequencies Occurring at the Peak of the Intonation Contour Produced by One Informant (in Hz)*

Syllable nucleus	No. of occurrences	Fundamental frequency
i	105	183
ɪ	141	173
eᴵ	119	169
ɛ	94	166
æ	131	162
ə	109	164
a	75	163
ɔ	79	165
oᵁ	93	170
ʊ	28	171
u	74	182
aᵁ	35	159
aɪ	93	160
ɔɪ	16	163
ɝ	71	171
	Total: 1,263	Average: 169

*After Lehiste and Peterson, 1961.

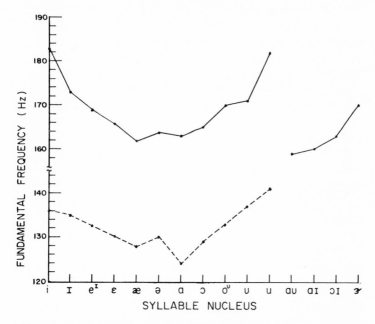

Figure 3.1. Average fundamental frequencies, in cycles per second, of syllable nuclei occurring at the peak of the intonation contour in 1263 test words (Lehiste and Peterson, 1961).

Barney (1952). Both graphs, but especially the upper one, resemble an acoustical vowel diagram, in which /i/ and /u/ are associated with the highest intrinsic fundamental voice frequencies; the open vowels, such as /a/ and /æ/, are associated with the lowest fundamental frequencies; and the central vowels, such as /ə/ and /ɝ/, occur approximately in the middle of the frequency range.

The fundamental frequency of diphthongs was, in this case, determined by the first component.

The differences associated with vowel quality appear quite large. There is no question but that they should be above the perceptual threshold for fundamental frequency. In this particular study, the test words all occurred on the same intonation level. In a linguistic analysis of intonation, it is thus necessary to allow for the fact that the same level is habitually associated with a variety of fundamental frequency values, varying in a manner that is influenced by the phonetic quality of the vowel. If a pitch level is considered phonemic, it must be kept in mind that its realization is determined to some extent by the segmental quality of the syllable nucleus over which it is realized.

The hypothesis that the high vowels such as [i] and [u] have relatively higher intrinsic pitch than lower vowels was tested by Ladefoged (1964a) by reference to Itsekiri, a West African tone language. Ladefoged found that high tone stems containing [i] and [u] had a peak fundamental frequency that was slightly more than 5 Hz higher than the mean peak high tone frequency relative to the frame; similarly, the fundamental frequency in the stems with mid and low tones was about 4 Hz higher when the vowel was [i] or [u]. These differences were clearly audible, but they were slightly less than those found by Lehiste and Peterson (1961). Ladefoged suggests that the discrepancy may not reflect a difference between English and Itsekiri, but rather that it may have been caused by a difference in the styles of speech of the informants, which may have been more emphatic or deliberate in the case of the English informant, and more colloquial in the case of the Itsekiri speaker. The fact remains that in both languages there is an observable effect of vowel quality on fundamental frequency.

There appears to be a physiological reason for the fact that high vowels are associated with a relatively high fundamental frequency. As was mentioned above, fundamental frequency increases with either increased rate of airflow or increased tension of the vocal folds (or a combination of the two). In the articulation of high vowels, the tongue is raised toward the roof of the mouth. Now, the muscles constituting the tongue are attached to the superior part of the hyoid bone, and some of the laryngeal muscles are attached to the inferior part. When the tongue is raised, the larynx tends to be pulled upwards and the laryngeal muscles are stretched. This increases the tension of the vocal folds and causes the increase in the rate of vibration.

Corroborative evidence is also available from Serbo-Croatian (Ivić and Lehiste, 1963). Table 3.4 shows average peak fundamental frequency values in the accented syllables of test words occurring in frame sentences, classified according to type of accent. The material reported in the table consisted of 875 test words produced by one speaker. The intrinsic pitch differences between high and low vowels in Serbo-Croatian are intermediate between those reported for English and Itsekiri.

An interesting fact in the Serbo-Croatian data is the low average fundamental frequency of syllabic /r/. In actual fact, the fundamental frequency fluctuated during the trill, decreasing during the closures and rising during the vocoidal parts. This fluctuation is due to physiological factors (probably to back pressure during the contact made by the tongue), as discussed earlier in Section 3.1.

3.4.2. Segmental conditioning factors The influence of preceding and following consonants on the average fundamental frequency of a syllable nucleus was likewise discussed by Lehiste and Peterson (1961). Figure 3.2 presents two curves, showing the fundamental frequency of the two vowels /i/ and /æ/ as a function of the initial consonant. These two vowels had the highest and the lowest intrinsic fundamental frequencies, respectively, in the set of words analyzed in the course of the study. The straight lines in the figure represent the average fundamental frequencies for /i/ (183 Hz) and /æ/ (162 Hz), computed for 105 occurrences of /i/ and 131 occurrences of /æ/.

As may be seen from the figure, higher fundamental frequencies occurred after a voiceless consonant and considerably lower fundamental frequencies occurred after a voiced consonant. The differences were quite large; for example, the average peak fundamental frequency of words beginning with the sequence /ti/ was 191 Hz, but of words beginning with /di/ it was 180 Hz; for /tæ/ and /dæ/, the average values were 175 and 158 Hz. The influence of an initial consonant could

Table 3.4. Average Fundamental Frequencies (F.F.) Occurring at the Peak of the Fundamental Frequency Contour Associated with Accented Vowels in a Set of 875 Serbo-Croatian Words Produced by One Informant (in Hz)*

Syllable nucleus	Short falling		Short rising		Long falling		Long rising		Total	Average
	No. of occurrences	Peak F.F.	No. of occurrences	Peak F.F.	No. of occurrences	Peak F.F.	No. of occurrences	Peak F.F.		
i	17	245	19	242	13	254	26	244	75	246
e	54	245	45	240	14	250	15	234	128	242
a	60	243	71	231	74	245	67	236	272	239
o	92	245	80	235	13	247	13	237	198	241
u	30	259	32	239	30	261	29	251	121	252
r	18	244	20	226	16	244	27	236	81	237
Total/ Average	271	247	267	236	160	250	177	240	875	243

* After Ivić and Lehiste, 1963.

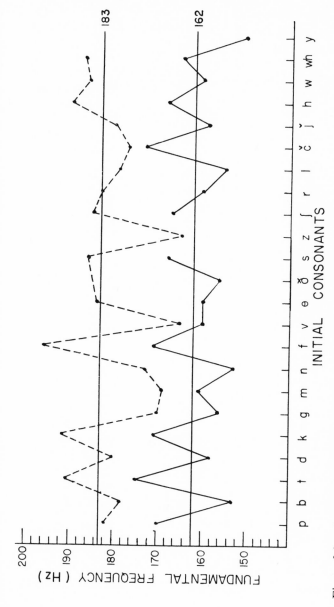

Figure 3.2. Average fundamental frequencies of 105 test words containing /i/ and 131 test words containing /æ/, arranged according to initial consonant. The solid lines show the average fundamental frequencies for all occurrences of /i/ and /æ/ (Lehiste and Peterson, 1961).

counterbalance the influence of intrinsic pitch: the average for /kæ/ sequences was 171 Hz, while that of /gi/ sequences amounted to 170 Hz.

The difference in average peak values due to the voicelessness or voicing of an initial consonant was accompanied by a different distribution of the fundamental frequency movement over the test word. After a voiceless consonant, and especially after a voiceless fricative, the highest peak occurred immediately after the consonant; whereas after a voiced consonant, especially a voiced resonant, the fundamental frequency rose slowly, and the peak occurred approximately in the middle of the test word. Wang reports (personal communication, 1969) that such segmental conditioning occurs also in tone languages with contour tones.

Final consonants showed no regular influence on the fundamental frequency of the syllable nuclei.

3.4.3. The dependence of tone upon phonation One obvious prerequisite for the distinctive functioning of fundamental frequency is the presence of phonation. An interesting problem in this context is the realization of tone in whispered speech. Whispering has certain effects on segmental sounds in addition to substituting a kind of breath noise (turbulence created at the glottis) for the glottal sound source. Whispered vowels have higher formant positions; this well-known fact is caused by the difference between the degree of openness of the glottis during phonation and whisper. During whisper, the glottis is incompletely closed; the vocal tract is excited by turbulent noise generated at the incompletely closed glottis. During phonation, the glottis may be considered effectively closed. The resonance frequencies of a tube open at both ends are higher than those of a tube closed at one end. Thus, the resonance frequencies of the vocal tract are higher when it is incompletely closed at the glottis.

In a study of whispered speech in English, I found that the first formant was approximately 200 to 250 Hz higher, and the second and third formants approximately 100 to 150 Hz higher, in whispered speech than in normally phonated speech (Lehiste,

1964b). In the same study I showed that the dynamic structure of English vowels differed in normally phonated and whispered speech. In phonated speech, the short simple syllable nuclei /ɪɛəu/ were characterized by a short target position and a long final transition; in whispered speech no such clear segmentation into target and final transition appeared possible. The transitional movement from the vowel target to the hub of the following consonant was much less prominent in whispered speech than in phonated speech. Sharf (1964) showed that in English, whispered vowels are noticeably longer than vowels in normally phonated words. Sharf grouped vowels in four sets according to intrinsic duration. The long vowels /æ, a, ɔ/ had average durations of 292 msec in normal speech and 356 msec in whispered speech; the relatively long vowels /e, ɝ, o/, 248 and 312 msec; the relatively short vowels /i, u/, 220 and 282 msec; and the short vowels /ɪ, ɛ, ə, ʊ/, 185 and 238 msec. Thus, whispered vowels were longer by an average duration of 60 msec. Sharf also found that the distinction in length conditioned by the voicing of the following consonant was maintained in whispered English: in his study, the duration ratio of vowels preceding voiceless consonants to those preceding voiced consonants was 0.56 for normal speech and 0.59 for whispered speech.

Meyer-Eppler (1957) showed that in German, intonational signals were preserved in whispered speech; however, their acoustic correlates were segmental rather than suprasegmental and consisted of shifts of some formant regions accompanied by added noise between higher formants.

There is ample evidence that at least in some tone languages, whispered words are intelligible. Hadding-Koch (1961) reported results of listening tests with spoken and whispered tones in several dialects of Swedish. Table 3.5 presents the relative intelligibility of whispered tones in five dialects. Hadding-Koch's results indicate that some dialects of Swedish lend themselves better to whispered word tones than others. It is not immediately obvious which of the many concomitant factors functions significantly in the absence of fundamental

Table 3.5. Results of Listening Tests with Spoken and Whispered Swedish Tones*

	Correct identifications†	
Dialect area	Spoken words	Whispered words
Skåne	99	50
Stockholm-Uppsala	98	66
Värmland	95	82
Göteborg	91	72
Ångermanland	86	85

* After Hadding-Koch, 1961, pp. 70–71.
† In % of total number of responses given for each dialect.

frequency in those dialects in which whispered tones are nearly as well identifiable as spoken tones. It might be assumed that intensity carries the main distinction; however, this seems unlikely in view of the fact that Hadding-Koch found it impossible to identify the spoken accents from the intensity curves alone.

Wang (1968b) has reported that the continuous amplitude contours of the four tones of Mandarin Chinese are very similar whether the syllables are voiced or whispered. There is some evidence that tonal oppositions in Chinese may be neutralized in whispered speech. Wise and Chong (1957) asked six informants to repeat a total of 3,824 whispered Chinese utterances. The informants repeated the critical words (in which tonal contrasts were present in normal phonation) with the correct tones 2,391 times and with incorrect tones 1,433 times, thus making correct identifications in 62% of the instances. If all four tones had been equally probable, the subjects theoretically would have been able to make correct identifications only 25% of the time. It is not clear from the study whether some tones were less subject to neutralization, or whether the 62% score could have been influenced by the fact that not all of the possible meanings of the words were equally suitable in the context of the sentences.

Kloster-Jensen (1958) tested the recognition of word tones in whispered Norwegian, Swedish, Slovene, and Mandarin

Chinese. He used a rather small group of speakers, and the results are probably not conclusive, but they provide some basis for a comparison between languages. Kloster-Jensen found that word tones were somewhat better reflected in whispered Swedish and Chinese than in Norwegian and Slovene. He also found that there were considerable individual differences in the effectiveness of a speaker; some subjects were clearly more intelligible than others who were whispering in the same language. Kloster-Jensen tested all four Mandarin tones against one another and found no systematic differences in their relative intelligibility.

Miller (1961) tested word tone recognition in Vietnamese whispered speech. Of 840 required identifications, his listeners identified 350 tones correctly, for a recognition score of 42%. In addition to confirming the observation that listeners differ in their ability to produce contrasts in whisper, Miller also found that there were some systematic substitutions. For example, low falling tone was often interpreted as low dipped, but not vice versa; the same applied to mid level, high broken, and low rising, all of which were frequently identified as low dipped. On the other hand the following tones were frequently substituted for each other: high broken and low rising, low rising and low falling, mid level and high rising. Miller concludes that very little word tone is transmitted in Vietnamese whispered speech.

More research is called for to decide the extent to which tonal features are intelligible in the absence of fundamental frequency, and to identify the phonetic features that are used to indicate the nature of the accent in whispered speech.

3.4.4. Phonetic quality and tone As was described in Section 3.4.1, vowels have intrinsic pitch: the phonetic quality of a vowel has a predictable influence on the fundamental frequency at which a given tonal feature may be realized. Intrinsic pitch appears to be a physiologically conditioned universal. Languages differ, however, with respect to the possible influence of tone on phonetic quality.

In tone languages with which I have worked, especially

Serbo-Croatian, tone appears to have no effect on phonetic quality. Figure 2.2, presented in the previous chapter, contains an acoustical vowel diagram in which the syllable nuclei are plotted separately for the four accents. It is clear from a study of the diagram (and from comparable data for twelve additional speakers; Lehiste and Ivić, 1963) that the tonal component of the accent has no influence on vowel quality, whereas the quantity component plays an important part in determining it.

However, in her study of Vietnamese vowels, Han (1966) found that one of the tones had a systematic influence on the position of the first formant of the vowels over which it was manifested. This tone was the "drop tone," which is characterized by a feature Han calls glottal constriction. (On spectrograms that she has published, the acoustic effect of glottal constriction looks very much like laryngealization.) The influence of the tone varied with the syllable nucleus and was stronger for high and mid vowels than for low vowels. The influence on the second formant was negligible. Table 3.6 contains a comparison of F_1 positions under the level tone and the drop tone for two informants.

Table 3.6. Average F_1 Positions of Vietnamese Vowels Bearing the Level Tone and the Drop Tone (in Hz)*

| Syllable nucleus | Average F_1 positions | | | | Difference between drop tone and level tone | |
| | Level tone | | Drop tone | | | |
	Speaker I	Speaker II	Speaker I	Speaker II	Speaker I	Speaker II
/i/	388	330	456	390	+68	+60
/e/	493	460	636	626	+143	+166
/ɯ/	448	429	545	510	+97	+81
/u/	398	377	463	434	+65	+57
/ɛ/	579	639	639	685	+60	+46
/ə/	595	553	711	748	+116	+195
/o/	531	511	576	573	+45	+62
/ʌ/	686	683	741	730	+55	+47
/ɔ/	652	660	663	679	+11	+19
/a/	771	850	794	854	+23	+4
/A/	801	805	778	893	−23	+88

* After Han, 1966, pp. 92–94.

Wang (1968b) reports that in the Foochow dialect of Chinese, high tones morphophonemically raise vowels from low to mid and from mid to high. This type of morpho-phonemic conditioning differs from strictly phonetic con-ditioning; one is led to assume, however, that a stage with allophonic raising of the vowels under high tones may have preceded the present stage. The lowering of vowels in Vietna-mese (higher F_1 positions are correlated with a lower tongue position) points toward a similar process.

3.4.5. Magnitude and kind of relevant differences   Relatively little information seems to be available concerning the allo-phonic variation permitted within a tonal system. Descriptions of manifestations of tone or intonation in natural speech usually indicate that areas of overlap were present within the ranges of a particular feature. It is not impossible that in two words presumably differing in tone, the fundamental frequency differences may happen to be minimal, while concomitant features of intensity, quantity, or segmental quality may carry the chief distinctive burden.

Experiments with synthetic speech provide an opportunity to test the relevant parameters separately. But the results of such tests are to be taken with a good deal of caution, precisely for the reason that in normal speech it is impossible to keep all other factors constant and to vary only one factor, such as the fundamental frequency of phonation. It is quite likely, for example, that in the absence of concomitant intensity differ-ences in the synthetic stimuli, a larger fundamental frequency difference is necessary for distinguishing between two tones than one finds in measurements made of actual utterances. One might then easily be led to disregard the actually occurring fundamental frequency differences altogether.

Synthetic speech has been used by Abramson (1961, 1962) to test the perception of synthetic tones in Thai. Abramson found that the tones were identifiable in isolated monosyllables. Highly intelligible tones could be synthesized using the average pitch contours that emerged from measurements of real speech. In the perception of tones, pitch convincingly overrode the effects of concomitant phonetic features observed in the utterances, such as variations in intensity, vowel quality, and duration. The fundamental frequency differences that produced a change in listener judgments were of the order of 5 Hz within a frequency range of 120 to 150 Hz.

Another aspect that lends itself to experimental manipulation is the duration of the syllable nucleus or word over which a tonal pattern is manifested. Efremova, Fintoft, and Ormestad (1965) studied the perception of tones in Norwegian by manipulating the duration of stressed first syllables of minimal pairs and presenting them to 95 listeners. The results show that the members of minimal pairs were identified with 90% accuracy when approximately 200 msec of the stressed vowel was included with the initial consonant, regardless of the original duration of the vowel. The authors conclude that the distinction between the accents is connected with the stressed syllable, and particularly with its tonal contour. Interestingly, a subset of their listeners, those with training in classical music, achieved a significantly higher recognition score than the rest of the listeners, who had little or no formal training in music.

The results of this experiment with Norwegian suggest that Norwegian accents are perceivable when only a fraction of the stressed syllable is presented; it was apparently not necessary to hear the whole sequence of syllables that is ordinarily assumed to constitute the domain of the accent (cf. Section 3.5.1). Exactly the opposite seems to be the case in Serbo-Croatian. In a brief experiment (Lehiste and Ivić, 1963), a series of listening tests was prepared and administered to two informants in which only the first syllables of minimally contrastive disyllabic words with short rising and short falling accents were presented for identification. When the intervocalic consonant was eliminated together with the nucleus of the second syllable, identifications were completely random. When a voiced intervocalic consonant was included in the truncated test words, identification became much better than chance. Inclusion of the complete second syllable resulted in complete identification. These listening tests support the notion that the domain of the accents in Serbo-Croatian includes the stressed and the immediately posttonic syllable.

Musical notation is used in a number of writings dealing with tone languages, and fundamental frequency movements are frequently expressed in terms of musical intervals. There is some advantage in using musical notation, since this makes it possible to discount the differences in individual ranges; however, it is questionable whether the relatively irregular fundamental frequencies of vocal fold vibration in speech are really perceived in the same way as musical tones. I carried through a small comparison between intonation contours in English and tonal contours in Norwegian, trying to establish whether a significant number of "pure" musical intervals were used in either language (Lehiste and Peterson, 1960).

For the purposes of this study, a musically "pure" interval was defined as the difference between two fundamental frequencies that can be expressed as a simple numerical ratio: 2/1 for an octave, 3/2 for a pure fifth, 4/3 for a pure fourth, 5/4 for a major third, 6/5 for a minor third, and so forth. An intonation pattern was considered to represent a "pure" interval when the ratio between the two frequency values did not differ from that of a "pure" interval by more than 1/100.

In English, the average frequency ratios on test words occurring at the peak of an intonation contour applied to a frame utterance differed considerably for different speakers. The intervals, expressed as fractions, ranged from 1.27 to 1.79; the first value falls between a major third and a pure fourth, the second between a minor and major seventh. The percentage of pure intervals ranged from 14 to 30% for the six speakers who served as subjects.

Of two Norwegian informants, one produced 53% pure intervals, the other 57%. The percentage of pure intervals involving a very simple frequency ratio (3, 4, 5, 6, and 8) for the two Norwegians was 49%. These data are, of course, very limited; nevertheless, it appears interesting that the same measuring technique applied to the two language samples revealed approximately twice as great a percentage of pure intervals in a tone language as compared to an intonation language. The fact that musically trained listeners performed better in identifying Norwegian tones may have some relevance in this connection; however, very little is known about the fluctuation in fundamental frequency within which a listener may identify a pitch movement with a specific musical interval, particularly when this interval occurs in speech.

3.4.6. Suprasegmental conditioning factors The supraseg-mental feature currently under consideration is practically independent of quantity but exhibits a high degree of inter-dependence with stress.

There is no evidence, to my knowledge, that greater length of a segment would automatically result in either higher or lower fundamental frequency. Likewise, there is no evidence that the occurrence of either high or low tones on a syllable would automatically entail either lengthening or shortening of the phonological element carrying the tone. The only interaction between tone and quantity appears to be distribu-tional: in many languages, contrastive tone appears only on long syllables. Such languages include Lithuanian (Ekblom, 1925; but cf. Robinson, 1968) and Serbo-Croatian (Ivić and Lehiste, 1963, 1965, 1967).

Stress, on the other hand, is frequently associated with higher fundamental frequency. The conditioning seems to proceed from stress to fundamental frequency. As was dis-cussed above, one of the factors causing the rate of vocal fold vibration to increase is increased rate of airflow. Since stress has been shown to be associated with increased subglottal pressure, the increase in vocal fold vibration may be considered automatic. If no increase is registered, it must be assumed that other adjustments are made (for example, in the tension of the vocal folds) to counteract the influence of the airflow. The matter will be discussed in more detail in Chapter 4.

There are two ways in which tonal features may constitute conditioning factors for other tonal features. Either the occurrence of tone on a syllable (or word) or its phonetic realization may be influenced by the presence or type of tone on an adjacent syllable (or word). This phenomenon is well known under the name *tone sandhi*. The other phenomenon involves fundamental frequency functioning at two levels, word level and sentence level, and consists of the fact that the realization of tones in a tone language may be influenced by intonation applied to the sentence as a whole. The latter case is analogous to the influence of tempo on quantity. Both tone sandhi and the interaction between tone and intonation will be discussed in the next section.

3.5. Fundamental frequency as independent variable

Contrastive function of fundamental frequency at word level is called *tone*; the term *intonation* refers to the linguistically significant functioning of fundamental frequency at the sentence level. I should like to distinguish between lexical tone, grammatical tone, and morphemic tone, although it may be necessary to collapse the latter two categories. *Lexical tone* is found in languages in which contrastive tone is associated with differences in the meanings of roots and stems (independently of stem formatives). Among such languages are Chinese and Slovene. *Grammatical tone* is a term I should like to apply to instances in which a difference in tone signals a difference in grammatical function without changing the lexical meaning or overt morphological structure. For example, the difference between dative and locative in a large group of Serbo-Croatian words is signaled by the occurrence of falling tone on the stem syllable in the dative and rising tone on the same syllable in the locative; the phonetic shape of the dative-locative suffix is identical. I would like to use the term *morphemic tone* in instances in which the tone on a root is predictable from the presence of a suffix morpheme, which need not carry the tone overtly. The predictable tone is realized only when the root is combined with the suffix; thus it is an inherent property of the suffix. The distinction between lexical tone and morphemic tone appears to be clear in Norwegian (Rischel, 1963). However, for the purposes of this chapter, the differences between lexical, grammatical, and morphemic tone are largely irrelevant.

3.5.1. The domain of tone The smallest possible domain of tone is a single syllabic sound. While it is certainly possible that a tone may be realized over a single segment in syllables containing just one voiced syllabic sound—one vowel preceded and followed by a voiceless consonant—it has been argued persuasively that the proper domain of tones is a syllable (Wang, 1967). Languages seem to differ with respect to the distribution of the fundamental frequency contour over the voiced portion of the syllable. In English, for example, the whole fundamental frequency movement of a terminal falling intonation produced on a word such as *feel* takes place on the vowel /i/, and the fundamental frequency levels off abruptly for the final /l/ (Peterson and Lehiste, 1960). I have analyzed the speech of a deaf subject who had obviously been taught to produce the falling intonation contour but who had not learned to distribute it over the vowel and consonant, respectively, in the manner characteristic of English. This subject produced the word *feel* with a fundamental frequency movement that continued into the final /l/; the result sounded nonnatural and nonnative. On the other hand, in languages such as Lithuanian the fundamental frequency contour clearly includes both a vowel and a postvocalic resonant.

In his masterly analysis of tone languages, Pike (1948) defined a tone language as having lexically significant, contrastive, but relative pitch on each syllable. Pike would exclude from tone languages proper such languages in which the domain of tonal patterns is larger than a single syllable (altogether he admits that tone languages may have tonemes distributed over polysyllabic roots). Pike includes Swedish, Norwegian, and Japanese among languages with what he calls "word-pitch" systems.

It appears that it might be profitable to distinguish between tonal patterns that are distributed over a disyllabic sequence and those that are the property of words (even though the words may be disyllabic). There are also languages in which a tonal pattern may be realized over a phrase. In the following discussion, examples will be drawn from three languages with which I am somewhat familiar: Swedish, Norwegian, and Serbo-Croatian. In each of these languages, pitch and stress features form a composite, which will be designated by the term *accent*.

According to Elert (1964), there are limitations in the occurrence of the Swedish tonal accents relative to the occurrence of word boundaries and of syllables with higher and lower levels of stress. The domain of accent II is at least disyllabic; the accent occurs only in polysyllabic words in which the syllable with a higher level of stress is followed by another syllable with a higher level of stress (as, for instance, in compound words) or by one or more syllables with a lower level of stress. The domain cannot contain a word boundary. When the domain of accent II includes two syllables with higher levels of stress, the syllables in between, if any, are included also. Accent I is not a word accent in the same sense as accent II; there is no prosodic contrast between an accent I word and a sequence of monosyllabic words or of polysyllabic accent I words.

In some Swedish and Norwegian dialects, as well as in Standard Norwegian of southeastern Norway, accent II may also be realized over phrases consisting of a verb + prepositional adverb or a verb + adverb or pronoun (Rischel, 1963; Vanvik, 1963). As in Swedish, both Norwegian accents are claimed to require at least a disyllabic sequence for their contrastive realization (but cf. Section 3.4.5, discussion of Efremova, Fintoft, and Ormestad, 1965).

While the domain of the Swedish marked accent (accent II) thus coincides with a lexical unit, in Norwegian the domain of the accent depends simultaneously on phonological and syntactic factors: accent II requires for its realization at least two syllables (phonological units), but of disyllabic sequences that are not parts of the same word, only certain syntactically determined phrases qualify as potential domains. The situation is different in Serbo-Croatian.

The remarks concerning Serbo-Croatian, presented here and later in this chapter, are based mainly on research carried on since 1961 in cooperation with Pavle Ivić (Lehiste, 1961; Lehiste and Ivić, 1963; Ivić and Lehiste, 1963, 1965, 1967; and as yet unpublished materials). As described in detail in the cited publications, the realization of the marked (rising) accent in Standard Serbo-Croatian requires a disyllabic sequence. As in Swedish and Norwegian, monosyllabic words do not show tonal contrasts. The distinction between short rising and short falling accent is realized in words of two or more syllables as a difference in the fundamental frequency of the posttonic syllable, which is higher in the words with rising accents than in words with falling accents. There is no fundamental frequency distinction in the accented short syllable itself. In words with long accents, the same difference appears in the second syllable; in addition, there is a difference in the fundamental frequency contour on the accented long syllable, which is falling in the case of the long accent and level or slightly rising in the long rising accent. In words with all accent types, the posttonic syllables may be followed by a number of further syllables with no contrastive fundamental frequency features.

Figure 3.3 illustrates the word-level patterns that occur in Serbo-Croatian. The figure contains curves drawn to represent the fundamental frequency movements during the syllable nuclei of 633 individual occurrences of test words with twelve accentual patterns, produced by one informant.

In general, the disyllabic sequence that constitutes the domain of the contrastive accentual patterns in Serbo-Croatian constitutes part of the same word; there are, however, a few instances in which certain proclitics may form an accentual unit with a following word, which in turn loses its separate accent and becomes part of the larger accentual unit. In Serbo-Croatian the disyllabic sequence that serves as the domain of contrastive (rising) fundamental frequency contours may not be broken up by unstressed or tonally neutral syllables, as is possible in Swedish.

3.5.2. Linguistic analysis of tone An interesting and largely successful attempt to integrate tonal features into an expanded

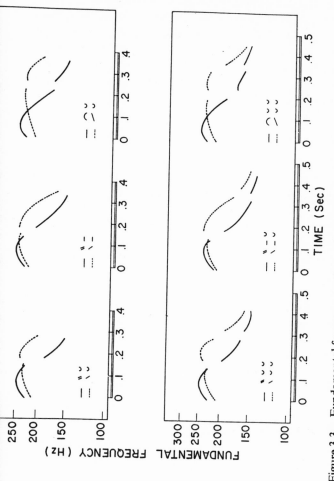

Figure 3.3. Fundamental frequency patterns observed in 12 Serbo-Croatian word types. Solid lines indicate contours associated with falling accents; dotted lines represent rising accents (Lehiste and Ivić, 1963, Figure 1).

distinctive features system has been made recently by Wang (1967). Wang suggests that, at least in some respects, tone features can be treated in the same way as segmental features, although phonetically the domain of tonal features is the syllable. He supports the latter claim with observations that in languages such as Chinese the tone features are sometimes relevant for the initial consonant, sometimes for the nuclear vowel, and sometimes for the final consonant in various phonological rules. If a column of tone features were to be added to a phonological matrix of segmental features, an arbitrary decision would have to be made of precisely where to insert this column. Furthermore, segmental features are usually not relevant in the various types of tone sandhi; the interaction of tones in a sequence is independent of the nature of the segments over which the tones are realized.

Wang proposes seven binary features—three level features and four features involving change of level. The seven binary features can, in principle, distinguish between 128 tones; Wang proposes that only 13 tones may be necessary to account for all the possibilities occurring in various tone languages. A survey of Wang's tonal features is given in Table 3.7. The top row of the table presents 13 tones, designated by "tone letters" proposed for the notation of tone by Y. R. Chao (1930).

Table 3.7.   Tones and Their Features*

Tonal features	Tones												
	1	2	3	4	5	6	7	8	9	10	11	12	13
CONTOUR	−	−	−	−	−	+	+	+	+	+	+	+	+
HIGH	+	−	+	−	−	+	−	+	−	+	−	+	−
CENTRAL	−	−	+	+	+	−	−	−	−	−	−	−	−
MID	−	−	−	−	+	−	−	−	−	−	−	−	−
RISING	−	−	−	−	−	+	+	−	−	+	+	+	+
FALLING	−	−	−	−	−	−	−	+	+	+	+	+	+
CONVEX	−	−	−	−	−	−	−	−	−	−	−	+	+

* From Wang, 1967.

Tones 1 through 5 indicate five distinctive pitch levels. Tones 6 through 9 are falling and rising tones; tones 10 through 13 involve a fall and rise within the same syllable.

The seven tonal features—contour, high, central, mid, rising, falling, and convex—make it possible to express the 13 tones as combinations of feature specifications in a manner similar to the specification of segmental phonemes. (The dotted lines in Table 3.7 enclose feature specifications that would be necessary if all 13 tones were lexically distinctive in a language; all remaining feature specifications of the table could then be predicted by redundancy conventions.) The −CONTOUR tones (i.e., tones 1 through 5) are divided into five levels by the features HIGH, CENTRAL, and MID. The +CONTOUR tones go either in one direction or in two directions; tones 6 through 9 are either +RISING or +FALLING, and tones 9 through 13 are both +RISING and +FALLING. The bidirectional tones are further divided by the feature CONVEX.

Wang (1968a) reports that in a recent survey of several hundred tone systems, he has found very few languages to have more than (1) four noncontour tones, (2) two rising tones, (3) two falling tones, or (4) two turning tones.

Wang's system of 13 tones fails to provide for the use of laryngealization in a tonal system. There are at least three languages that I know of in which one of the tones is associated with a modification of the phonatory process described earlier as laryngealization. In Danish, the opposition is between presence and absence of this glottal modification (Hansen, 1943; Smith, 1944). The glottal modification, usually referred to by its Danish name *stød*, cannot be analyzed as a glottal stop, because there are some dialects in which *stød* contrasts with a glottal stop (Ringgaard, 1960, 1962). In Vietnamese, two of the tones are usually associated with a glottal constriction. According to spectrograms published by Han (1966), they differ in the placement of this glottal constriction: the "broken tone" has a period of laryngealization in the first half of the syllable nucleus, while the "drop tone" ends with a period of laryngealization.

In Latvian, laryngealization is the one consistent phonetic feature associated with the so-called third tone. In a recent study (Lehiste, 1968b), I compared Danish words with *stød* with Latvian words bearing the third tone. Whatever additional phonetic factors may be involved in the production of the *stød*, there is good acoustic evidence of the presence of laryngealization. The Latvian case is quite clear. Since laryngealization is produced by a modification of the phonatory process, it seems to be necessary to include it among possible tonal features. Laryngealization may, of course, also function noncontrastively as an allotone of low pitch, as an accompanying feature of falling intonation, or as a boundary signal.

Wang's first and basic distinction between −CONTOUR and +CONTOUR tones parallels the classification given by Pike (1948), who divided tonal systems into level-pitch register systems and gliding-pitch contour systems. In Pike's classification, the first type includes systems that are comprised largely of level tonemes—tonemes that are realized in such a manner that, within the limits of perception, the pitch of a syllable does not rise or fall during its production. The contrastive levels are called registers. Pike suggests that the number of permitted registers may be limited to four. Wang (1967) discusses some cases of five distinctive pitch levels, and provides for them by setting up the feature MID in his feature system.

One difference between the classificatory schemes of Wang and Pike consists of the fact that Pike distinguishes between true contours and apparent contours. The latter may occur in languages with register-tone systems if a single syllable carries more than one toneme. In these cases, the glides are to be analyzed in terms of their end points: the starting point of the glide is a toneme constituted of one of the level pitches, and the ending point is a toneme of one of the other levels. In bidirectional tones, the reversal point is a toneme of a third level, or starting and ending points may be one level and the reversal point a second level. Pike mentions Apache, Navaho, and Hausa among languages in which gliding tonal movements should best be analyzed as successions of levels with non-phonemic glides in between. Glides of this type may be parts of a single morpheme, as in Mixteco, or they may be interrupted by a morpheme boundary.

Gliding-pitch contour systems differ from register systems in a number of points: (1) the basic tonemic unit is gliding instead of level; (2) the unitary contour glides cannot be interrupted by morpheme boundaries as can the nonphonemic compounded types of a register system; (3) the beginning and ending points of the glides of a contour system cannot be equated with level tonemes in the same system, whereas all glides of a register system are to be interpreted phonemically in terms of their end points; and (4) contour systems have only one toneme per syllable, whereas some of the register-tone languages may have two or more tonemes per syllable. Contours may differ in many ways; the differences may include the following: (1) differences of direction (rising, falling, falling-rising, rising-falling, falling-rising-falling); (2) differences of beginning-point height (fall beginning low, fall beginning higher, rise beginning in between the two); (3) differences in beginning and ending points, none of which can be equated in height to any other or to level tonemes; (4) differences of distance (slight fall, greater fall, greatest fall); (5) differences of time (short time, longer time, longest time); (6) differences in correlation between the time and distance of rise (fast beginning rise with slow ending, slow beginning rise with fast ending); (7) differences in correlation with stress placement (greater intensity at the beginning of the rise, greater intensity at the end); and (8) differences in correlation with glottal stop (rise arrested abruptly with glottal stop, rise not so arrested).

Pike suggests further that there exist tone languages that do not fit completely either the register-tone class or the contour-tone class but combine elements of both systems. Sample combined systems might include two or more glides in the same direction but of different heights, with two or more level tonemes among the glides. Pike considers various languages of China among languages of a contour type with strong register overlap.

An obvious problem in Pike's classification is the distinction between true and apparent glides, i.e., contour tones and occurrences of two or more tonemes on a single syllable. Even if such a distinction should be necessary, it is difficult to establish nonarbitrary criteria for determining which of the two is present in a language. Pike solves the problem by proposing a distinction between phonetic and phonemic syllables (Pike, 1954–1960 [1967]); however, since part of Pike's evidence for syllables (Stetson, 1951) has been refuted by later experimental research (summarized in Ladefoged, 1967), the problem cannot be considered completely solved.

In establishing the number of contrastive tones in a language, noncontrastive variation has to be eliminated. The term *toneme* is frequently applied to contrastive elements in a tonal system. Jones (1950 [1962]) defines a toneme as a family of tones in a given tone language that count for linguistic purposes as if they were one and the same, the differences being due to tonal or other context.

It is a characteristic of many tone languages that the realization of a particular tone depends heavily upon the tones occurring on neighboring syllables. This phenomenon is known under the name *tone sandhi*. There are many ways in which tone sandhi may operate, and these may provide an additional basis for the classification of tone languages. Welmers (1959) has suggested a further division of register tone languages into discrete-level languages, such as Yoruba, and terraced-level languages, such as Twi. In Yoruba, the tones are always in the same relation to one another (for example, one high, one in the mid range, and one low), whereas in Twi the pitch of one of the tones depends on which of the other tones occurs immediately before it. There are three tonemes in Twi: high, high-change, and low (Schachter, 1961). The high and low tonemes show variation on the basis of a fixed contrastive relation in which each variant of a toneme has the highest or the lowest fundamental frequency that occurs in its position in a tonemic sequence. The high-change toneme shows variation on the basis of a fixed change relation. Tonemic variants sharing a fixed change relation have in common both a distinctive contrastive position and a distinctive sequential one. In Twi, two contrastive tones may occur in initial position: a low tone and a nonlow tone. Recurrent low pitches represent the low toneme. The nonlow tone, however, may be followed by two nonlow tones, one of which is at the same level (echo), the other at mid level (step-down). In noninitial positions, there are thus three possible contrasts. A mid level tone may again be followed by three levels: the same level as the mid tone, a lower level, and a low level. A nonlow tone may never be followed by a tone that has a higher pitch than the preceding tone; in a typical long phrase, an effect of terraced descent is heard. Schachter analyzes the tone that is always at the same level as the preceding tone as a high toneme, since it is the highest tone that may occur in its environment. The step-down tone is analyzed as a high-change tone. The reasons for the particular analysis are partly a desire to simplify the morphophonemics of Twi, and partly an attempt to preserve phonetic similarity among tonal variants that are assigned to one toneme.

The domain of the sandhi pattern just described appears to be the whole utterance that is bounded by pauses. In Chinese dialects, sandhi seems to be conditioned by syntactic boundaries, on the one hand, and speech tempo, on the other (Wang, 1967). A particularly interesting phenomenon of sandhi has been reported for Amoy Hokkien (Bodman, 1955; quoted in Wang, 1967). The seven lexical tones of this dialect may be specified by the four features HIGH, FALLING, RISING, and LONG in the manner indicated in Table 3.8. The numbers assigned to the tones correspond etymologically to the four tones of Middle Chinese; the letters a and b indicate a historical split that corresponds, respectively, to unvoiced and voiced initial consonants. In a large class of syntactic environments, the tones undergo sandhi in a way that can be symbolized by a tone circle and linearized in the following formula:

$$\begin{pmatrix} \text{Ia} \\ \text{Ib} \end{pmatrix} \rightarrow \text{IIIb} \rightarrow \text{IIIa} \rightarrow \text{II} \rightarrow \text{Ia}$$

Table 3.8. Tones of Amoy Hokkien

Tonal features	Tones						
	Ia	Ib	II	IIIa	IIIb	IVa	IVb
HIGH	+	+	+	−	−	−	+
FALLING	−	−	+	+	−	+	−
RISING	−	+	−	−	−	−	−
LONG	+	+	+	+	+	−	−

* After Wang, 1967.

Tone IV does not participate in the sandhi circle; in other words, the sandhi changes occur only in the environment +LONG. The neutralization of tones Ia and Ib in the sandhi position makes it possible to restate the formula in terms of only two phonological features:

$$\begin{bmatrix} +\text{HIGH} \\ -\text{FALLING} \end{bmatrix} \rightarrow \begin{bmatrix} -\text{HIGH} \\ -\text{FALLING} \end{bmatrix} \rightarrow \begin{bmatrix} -\text{HIGH} \\ +\text{FALLING} \end{bmatrix}$$

$$\rightarrow \begin{bmatrix} +\text{HIGH} \\ +\text{FALLING} \end{bmatrix} \rightarrow \begin{bmatrix} +\text{HIGH} \\ -\text{FALLING} \end{bmatrix}$$

This formulation makes the regularity of the alternations clearly apparent. Only one feature changes its specification in each alternation. If the two features of the basic tone have the same specification, then FALLING will change its specification; if the two features have opposite signs, HIGH will change its value. Thus, the HIGH feature of the derived tone takes on the same specification as the FALLING feature of the basic tone, while the FALLING feature of the derived tone takes on the opposite specification of the HIGH feature of the basic tone. In Wang's ingenious analysis, all four pair-wise alternations are captured by the single phonological rule:

$$\begin{bmatrix} \alpha\text{HIGH} \\ \beta\text{FALLING} \end{bmatrix} \rightarrow \begin{bmatrix} \beta\text{HIGH} \\ -\alpha\text{FALLING} \end{bmatrix}$$

In the literature with which I am familiar, occurrences of tone sandhi appear to be restricted to languages in which each syllable carries contrastive tone. Sentence intonation may affect the realization of tones both in tone languages of the type just described and in languages with word tones, such as Swedish and Serbo-Croatian. The interaction between tone and intonation will be discussed in Section 3.5.4.

3.5.3. Intonation The use of tonal features to carry linguistic information at the sentence level is one of the meanings of the term *intonation*. Intonation also carries nonlinguistic meanings; in this respect it is analogous to tempo, i.e., the use of features of duration at the sentence level to reflect the attitudes of the speaker and the relative urgency of the message. Many attempts have been made to separate the linguistic and attitudinal aspects of intonation (Uldall, 1960, 1964; Wodarz, 1962a; Hadding-Koch, 1961). The difficulties inherent in trying to achieve this separation become clear when one considers the results achieved by Hadding-Koch (1961). It was not possible to correlate grammatical sentence types and intonation contours. There was no special question intonation; questions were normally characterized by an elevated intonation level rather than by a special contour. The elevated intonation level, however, was shared by several types of sentences that the author classified as "reactions" of the speakers. A further interaction appeared between the intonation contour and the lexical content of the sentence. The same contour was often interpreted differently, depending on the verbal content of the utterance and the context in which it appeared. A contour that was interpreted as "neutral" in one context became an indication of indifference when the situation required greater interest or friendliness to cover the meaning of the words adequately. In utterances with no particular pointing or interest, the same contour could be interpreted as neutral, without any suggestion of indifference. In further sentences, the use of the same contour was considered "negative" by the listeners: evidently, the attitude implied by the contour was not sufficiently "lively" to suggest an ordinary, neutral answer in that particular context.

As far as the interpretation of the speakers' attitudes was concerned, the listeners showed a very small degree of agreement among themselves as to what the intended attitude of the speaker might have been.

While there is agreement among researchers that linguistic and attitudinal aspects have to be kept separate, there is no effective and universally applicable methodology for achieving this separation. In the following discussion, it will be assumed that it is possible to deal with the linguistic function of intonation alone; this assumption seems to underlie most published work on the linguistic aspects of intonation.

Intonation does not change the meaning of lexical items, but constitutes part of the meaning of the whole utterance; certain changes in intonation may be accompanied by changes in the function of the utterance, signaling, for example, a difference between a statement or a question. There is some difference of opinion regarding the manner in which intonation features are used to achieve this means. In the analysis of English intonation, there have been two schools of thought: those proposing that intonations should be specified in terms of a number of pitch levels (Wells, 1945; Pike, 1945; Trager and Smith, 1951) and those suggesting a number of significant contours or pitch configurations (most British linguists, including Armstrong and Ward, 1926; Palmer, 1922; Kingdon, 1958; and, among American linguists, Bolinger, 1958). The smallest units of intonation are either the "phonemic pitch levels," of which Wells, Pike, and Trager and Smith postulate four, or "tone groups" (Palmer, 1922) or "tunes" (Armstrong and Ward, 1926). The pitch phonemes (i.e., the phonemic pitch levels) are organized into pitch morphemes that are strict analogies of segmental morphemes composed of segmental phonemes. The pitch morphemes also have the function of indicating the immediate constituent structure of the utterance (Wells, 1947).

Bolinger (1958) rejects the phonemic function of the four pitch levels of Wells, Pike, and Trager and Smith, and presents experimental evidence that it is the movement of the melody, its configuration, which bears the meaning of intonation. In spite of the apparent mutual exclusiveness of the two points of view, it nevertheless appears probable that both levels and configurations have to be specified for certain purposes.

Hadding-Koch (1961) examined the possibility of analyzing Swedish in terms of a modified Trager-Smith system, with four distinctive pitch levels and three terminal junctures. Plotting the highest and lowest points of frequency used by her speakers on a musical scale, she found that all speakers had certain "favorite" frequency regions that were used recurrently in similar circumstances. There were one or, more often, two main concentrations of items at higher frequencies, one intermediate area with few occurrences, and one or two concentrations on frequencies below this comparatively empty area. The pitch levels discovered by this procedure seemed to have some absolute rather than merely relative significance: the pitch levels established in this manner for two of the speakers remained more or less the same when the experiment was repeated after a lapse of 18 months.

Commenting upon Hadding-Koch's results, Lieberman (1967) has suggested that the clustering around certain frequencies may be connected with the fact that normal speakers tend to avoid phonation at fundamental frequencies that seem to correspond to (or excite) the resonances of the subglottal system (cf. Section 3.1). The "phonemic" pitch levels may merely reflect the phonetic effect of the discontinuities caused by the coupling of the subglottal system to the larynx.

The possibility of physiological and acoustic conditioning of pitch levels leads to the question of whether there are any universal physiologically definable correlates of specific intonational features. Lieberman (1967) has stated that intonation is produced and perceived in terms of an unmarked and a marked breath-group and certain segmental features that interact with the breath-group because of the inherent constraints imposed by the human speech production apparatus and auditory system. The breath-group is a suprasegmental feature whose scope is usually a sentence. At the articulatory level, the breath-group involves a coordinated pattern of muscular activity that includes the subglottal, laryngeal, and supraglottal muscles during an entire expiration. At the end of the sentence, the subglottal respiratory muscles lower the subglottal air pressure during the last 150 to 200 msec of phonation. For the unmarked American English breath-group, the tension of the laryngeal muscles appears to remain relatively steady throughout the sentence. The fundamental frequency of phonation is thus a function of the subglottal air pressure, and it falls during the last 150 to 200 msec of phonation. The marked breath-group contrasts with the unmarked breath-group during the last 150 to 200 msec of phonation; the tension of the laryngeal muscles increases in the marked breath-group during this terminal phase. The increased tension of the laryngeal muscles counters the falling subglottal air pressure, and the marked breath-group thus has a terminal nonfalling fundamental frequency contour. On the basis of an analysis of the cries of newborn infants, Lieberman claims that the unmarked breath-group is innately determined; the falling terminal fundamental frequency contour is apparently a universal aspect of the unmarked breath-group.

This hypothesis has been recently challenged. Ohala and Hirano (1967) made electromyographic studies of the activity during speech of lateral cricoarytenoid, cricothyroid and sternohyoid muscles. The vocalis and interarytenoid muscles were also sampled for one subject, and direct recordings were obtained of the subglottal pressure. The cricothyroid and lateral cricoarytenoid assist in raising pitch, and the sternohyoid assists in lowering pitch. The data provided no confirmation of Lieberman's hypothesis that, for American English, during other than yes-no questions, the laryngeal tension remains relatively steady and that pitch variation is a function of the subglottal air pressure. On the contrary, the muscles studied participated actively in pitch control, and variations in subglottal pressure could account for only a fraction of the observed pitch changes. Lieberman's model thus needs to be modified before it can serve as basis for a physiologically based theory of intonation.

The question of the universality of intonation has been considered, and answered affirmatively, by Bolinger (1964).

Bolinger found universality in the tension-relaxation dichotomy, which he assumes to rest on the psychophysical makeup of the human race. He suggests that the only indefectibly universal aspect of fundamental pitch is its association with the muscular tension of the whole organism. Emotional tension is reflected in tension of the vocal folds, which automatically raises pitch. The mere effort of speaking increases subglottal pressure, which also raises pitch, and provides a purely physiological explanation for higher pitch in the early part of an utterance and lower pitch toward the end, even when there is no pitch rise due to excitement. Excitement, besides pitching high the entire length of an agitated utterance, gives us the rudiments of an accent system in which the pitch goes up only on the items that are exciting. Unfinished business, besides telling us that we are in the middle of an utterance, next transfers the high pitch of the middle to the end, enabling us to leave things such as questions deliberately unfinished for the interlocutor to finish them. High terminal pitch for unfinished business is primary; rising pitch for questions is secondary. An accent language employing relative heights may distinguish old from new or topic from comment, with intonation getting a foothold in the syntax.

A recent survey of research on intonation has been given by Magdics (1963). There is a considerable amount of new information not treated by Magdics, both experimental and descriptive, about the functioning of intonation in various languages. An incomplete list might include Wodarz (1960, 1962b, 1963), Delattre (1962b), Denes and Milton-Williams (1963), Magdics (1964), Rigault (1964), Hadding-Koch and Studdert-Kennedy (1964, 1965), Gårding and Abramson (1965), Fónagy (1965), and many others. Attempts have also been made to define the role of intonation in generative grammar (Stockwell, 1960; Isačenko and Schädlich, 1966; Bierwisch, 1966). It is impossible to review all the relevant material within the present framework. I should like to consider next the interrelation between tone and intonation in tone languages.

3.5.4. Interaction between tone and intonation If intonation
is indeed a linguistic universal, it should be present also in tone
languages. While admitting that all tone languages have
intonation of the emotional type, Pike (1948) doubted whether
they have highly organized contrastive systems with a limited
number of relative levels controlling the formation of intonations that carry shades of meaning. Bolinger (1964), in his
study of the universality of intonation, was able to find only
one language (Amahuaca) in which no system of intonation
had been found, although fluctuations of pitch or overall level
of the utterance due to emotion were present. In a wide
variety of tone languages, however, intonation patterns of one
kind or another have been reported. The influence of intonation upon tone may take different forms. According to
Bolinger (1964, and literature quoted there), in Lhasa Tibetan,
intonation takes over everywhere except in citation forms.
In Huichol, tonemes are found only in the intonational
precontour and are lost in the nuclear contour. Burmese loses
tonemic contrasts under some conditions. In Otomi, only the
last syllable of the word carries intonational pitches, while
preceding syllables carry tonemes. A similar situation prevails
in the Chengtu dialect of Szechuan (Chang, 1958), in which
intonation affects the pitch level at which the sentence is
spoken and the range of pitch the sentence covers, but does
not affect the realization of the tonemes except on the final
syllable (the tonemes, however, are subject to regular tone
sandhi rules everywhere in the sentence). A gradual down-
drift, distributed over the whole utterance, is very common in
many African languages (Schachter, 1961). The Acatlan
dialect of Mixtec constitutes a terrace-level language of the
ascending variety (Wang, 1967, and 1968b, based on unpublished materials of E. Pike and K. Wistram).

To illustrate some ways in which tone and intonation may
interact, I should like to consider in somewhat greater detail
the tone and intonation systems of Serbo-Croatian and
Swedish. The two systems have similarities as well as differences.

In Serbo-Croatian, the realization of word accents is strongly influenced by the intonation applied to the sentence as a whole. In addition, degrees of stress and emphasis play a part in the realization of the accents. Emphasis in statements tends to bring out an optimal (i.e., most clearly contrastive) realization of the accent; in yes-no questions, emphasis makes the appearance of a special "reverse" accent obligatory rather than optional. Without emphasis, words are closest to optimal accentual realization in the middle of the utterance, at the peak of a neutral intonation contour, which normally rises in the beginning of the utterance and falls gradually at the end of the utterance. In initial position, the rising and falling accents tend to be neutralized in the direction of rising accents; i.e., words with falling accents have a relatively high second syllable, which is a normal characteristic of rising accents. In final position, accents tend to be neutralized in the direction toward falling accents; words with rising accents acquire both a falling tonal contour on the stressed syllable and a low second syllable. Often the distinction between the accents is maintained through a different kind of phonetic means: disyllabic words with falling accents occurring in final position have a laryngealized second syllable, whereas words with rising accents have a final syllable phonated at the lowest level of the speaker's phonatory range.

Questions containing an interrogative adverb usually have the neutral intonation contour just described. Questions containing an interrogative particle may have two kinds of intonation contours: the neutral contour or a contour in which one of the words bears a special kind of neutralized accent. More often than not the accent appears on the verb; however, if emphasis is present, the word produced with emphasis also bears the special accent. Yes-no questions not containing an interrogative particle usually contain a word with the neutralized accent; in the case of emphasis, the neutralized accent is always present. The special accent is characterized by a low accented syllable and a high posttonic syllable. In most instances the fundamental frequency contour within the accented syllable is concave, but there are also instances of laryngealization and voicelessness of the accented syllable. The interval between the accented and posttonic syllable appears to be close to the limits of the speaker's range. The special accent, which we have called "reverse pattern," replaces both falling and rising accents; the contrast between them is completely neutralized.

There are thus two kinds of neutralizations of accents due to the influence of intonation. In nonemphatic sentence-initial and sentence-final position, the neutralization is toward one of the existing accents; in initial position, falling accents look more like rising accents, whereas in final position, rising accents assume the phonetic shape of falling accents. In yes-no questions, the word in focus receives a special "reverse" accent, which occurs nowhere else and which obliterates the inherent accentual differences of the words on which it appears.

Figure 3.4 contains reproductions of narrow-band spectrograms of two sentences, *Jȁgnje se dȁruje bȁbama?* 'Is the sheep given to the old women?' and *Za snȁšice je i trȁvica?* 'Is the grass also for the daughters-in-law?' In both sentences, the last word bears the neutralized "reverse" pattern; the short falling accent of *bȁbama* and the short rising accent of *trȁvica* appear indistinguishable.

An attempt to provide a quantitative model for word and sentence intonation has been made by Öhman (1967). The main features of the model are the following. The fundamental frequency signal is synthesized by a mechanism ("larynx model") that accepts three types of input: (1) the time-varying "vocal cord tension," which is the sum of two components, sentence intonation and word intonation; (2) an acoustic interaction signal arising from the secondary effects on fundamental frequency caused by fluctuations in subglottal and supraglottal pressure; and (3) an articulatory interaction signal deriving from the nonphonatory movements of the hyothyroid lever system, due to certain articulatory gestures of the tongue. The speech material for which the model has been developed consists mainly of noncompound Swedish

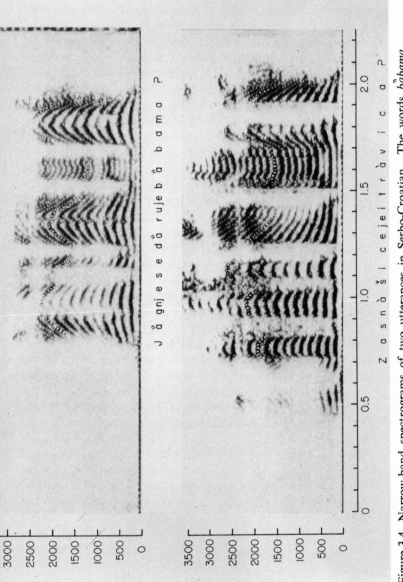

Figure 3.4. Narrow-band spectrograms of two utterances in Serbo-Croatian. The words *bȁbama* and *trȁvica* bear the neutralized "reverse" accent.

accented words embedded in two frames that provide two relatively unstressed syllables before and after the test word. Sentence intonation starts at a constant fundamental frequency. At the beginning of the first syllable of the accented word, a positive step is introduced into the sentence intonation filter. A second step of negative amplitude, representing the end contour, is added in the neighborhood of the penultimate syllable of the utterance. The word accents are represented by a negative pulse fed to the word intonation filter at a certain moment relative to the sentence intonation step. This moment is early for the acute accent (accent I) and late for the grave accent (accent II). From the addition of the positive intonation step and the negative word tone step, fundamental frequency contours may be generated that correspond to all Scandinavian tonal systems.

Öhman then interprets in physiological terms the model elements out of which the sentence intonation is built up. The word intonation pulse (negative amplitude step) appears to have a physiological correlate in the activity of the cricothyroid muscles; Öhman has found a brief phase of inhibition of cricothyroid activity at the moment when the negative word intonation pulses would occur for the two accents (early for the acute accent and late for the grave). The author proposes the hypothesis that the Scandinavian tonal accents are a sort of laryngeal consonants, not unlike glottal stops, that are coarticulated with the sentence intonation as well as with the segmental gestures of stressed syllables. The sentence intonation commands, on the other hand, can be decomposed into a basic phrase contour and a sequence of phonatory stress pulses. These constructs reflect an underlying process termed *physiological intensity;* stress should be understood as the addition of a quantum of physiological energy to the speech production system as a whole. This energy is distributed over the pulmonary, phonatory, and articulatory channels. In the phonatory channel, the stress energy manifests itself as a phonatory stress pulse at the input of the sentence intonation filter.

Öhman suggests that the intonation model he has developed might be applied to the description of other tone languages. It appears that the model should work, mutatis mutandis, for the Serbo-Croatian system presented earlier. The difference between word tones could be described in terms of a negative pulse, which is applied to the second syllable of a word with falling accent and not applied at all to a word with rising accent. The "reverse pattern" could be generated by applying the negative pulse to the accented syllable.

Öhman's model makes it possible to collect systematic quantitative information on the tonal as well as other prosodic events. It will be interesting to see whether intonation in other tone languages can likewise be described by means of a simple negative pulse fed to the input of the word intonation filter.

3.5.5. *Summary* The realization of tonal features may be conditioned by the following factors: individual variations in the size and shape of the phonatory apparatus; tension of the vocal folds; subglottal pressure; articulatory gestures of the tongue; coupling of the larynx to the vocal tract; degree of stress; tonal features appearing on adjacent syllables; and tonal features applied to the whole utterance. Fundamental frequency may function independently at word level (tone) and at sentence level (intonation). The domain of tone may be a syllable or a word; the domain of intonation patterns is the utterance. The possible analyses of tonal features include treatment of tonal features as distinctive features of tone whose domain is a syllable and treatment of tonal features as pitch phonemes (tonemes). At the sentence level, intonation may be described in terms of significant levels, in terms of contours, or as a combination of the two.

CHAPTER FOUR
STRESS

Of the three suprasegmental features considered in this study, stress has for a long time been the most elusive one. There is no single mechanism to which the production of stress can be attributed in the same manner as the generation of fundamental frequency can be attributed to the vibration of the vocal folds. Further, the points of view of the speaker and the hearer have often been confused in defining stress. When the speaker's activity in producing stressed syllables is in focus, stress may be defined in terms of greater effort that enters into the production of a stressed syllable as compared to an unstressed syllable. Jones (1950 [1962]), for example, defined a strongly stressed syllable as one that the speaker consciously utters with greater effort than other neighboring syllables in the word or sentence. When stress is defined from a listener's standpoint, the claim is often made that stressed syllables are louder than unstressed syllables (Bloomfield, 1933). Loudness can at least be tested through psychoacoustic techniques; but until recently, it has been practically impossible to measure effort. Experimental techniques developed during the last 15 years have nevertheless made it possible to establish some of the physiological correlates of linguistic stress. These will be discussed in the next section.

4.1. *Physiological mechanism involved in stress*

Ultimately, differences in stress are due to differences in physical effort. The effort is reflected directly in the activity of the muscles involved in respiration, and indirectly in subglottal pressure.

Direct evidence concerning the muscles involved in respiration can be obtained by means of the technique known as electromyography (Fromkin and Ladefoged, 1966). Using this technique, it is possible to record the electrical activity in a muscle that is generated when the muscle fibers contract. Two kinds of electrodes may be employed: surface electrodes, which are placed on the skin immediately above the muscles; and needle electrodes, which are inserted directly into the muscle. A great deal of our information regarding the relationships between respiratory activity and stress derives from electromyographic and related studies carried through by Peter Ladefoged and his co-workers (Ladefoged, Draper, and Whitteridge, 1958; Draper, Ladefoged, and Whitteridge, 1958, 1960; Ladefoged, 1960; Ladefoged, 1962b; Ladefoged and McKinney, 1963; Ladefoged, 1963, 1964b, reacting to Kunze, 1964; the material is summarized in Ladefoged, 1967). The following account is based largely on Ladefoged's work.

The main muscles involved in respiration are the external intercostals, the internal intercostals, and the diaphragm. The external intercostals and the diaphragm are muscles of inspiration; the internal intercostals are involved in expiration. The external intercostals are thin sheets of muscle linking the ribs to the fixated first rib, the vertebrae of the neck, and the base of the skull. When they contract, they lift the rib cage outward and thus expand the thoracic cavity. The diaphragm is a dome-shaped muscle attached to the ribs and spinal column that forms the base of the thoracic cavity. Its contraction expands the thoracic cavity downward and thus also increases its volume. The internal intercostals lie deeper than the external intercostals; their fibers run downward and backward and thus lie at an angle to the external intercostals. The internal intercostals constitute a sheet of muscles that, through other muscles, link the ribs to the pelvis. When they contract, they pull the ribs down, thus decreasing the size of the thoracic cavity. At the end of a long expiration, other muscles may enter into play to force air out of the lungs and to maintain constant subglottal pressure.

When the volume of the thoracic cavity and thus of the lungs increases, air pressure inside the lungs decreases and inspiration results. Conversely, when the volume of the thoracic cavity is decreased, pressure is exerted on the air in the lungs and expiration takes place. The force exerted by the muscles is transmitted to the air in the lungs and is reflected in the subglottal pressure. If linguistic stress is indeed connected with increased effort, differences in stress should be reflected in changes of subglottal pressure.

Various techniques have been developed for measuring subglottal pressure. These have been critically evaluated recently by Lieberman (1968). Basically, there are two methods. The direct method, as its name implies, involves direct measurement of air pressure inside the trachea. This can be done by inserting a hollow needle into the trachea below the glottis (Strenger, 1960). Van den Berg had previously used a catheter that was introduced through the glottis without impeding the movements of the vocal folds (van den Berg, 1956). The indirect method is based on the assumption that subglottal pressure can be estimated from esophageal pressure. In measuring subglottal pressure by means of this technique, a small rubber balloon, attached to the end of a tube, is inserted through the nose into the esophagus. The size of the balloon has varied in the different experiments from 3.5 to 10 cm in length; the diameter has been approximately 1.5 to 2 cm. When the balloon has been positioned at the desired level in the upper part of the esophagus, it is inflated (filled with from 2 to 5 ml of air); since the balloon rests firmly between the thin posterior membrane of the trachea and the vertebral column, any pressure changes in the trachea are transmitted to the air in the balloon. The pressure in the balloon is transmitted through the tube and recorded, using a pressure transducer, on an oscillograph or other suitable device. The interpretation of the records requires taking into account such factors as the volume of the lungs and differences between speakers in the elasticity of their lungs. Nevertheless, the indirect method has been developed to a point where it can provide fairly reliable estimates of subglottal pressure (Ladefoged, 1967; Lieberman, 1968).

Electromyographic studies of the activity of the internal intercostals during the repetition of a single stressed syllable show, first, that there is a general increase in the amount of muscular activity as the utterance proceeds, and second, that the muscular activity occurs mainly in bursts that immediately precede each syllable. The general increase in muscular activity can be correlated with the decrease in the volume of air in the lungs that takes place during the production of the utterance. Greater effort is required to maintain constant subglottal pressure toward the end of an expiration. The bursts of activity preceding each syllable in the production of a train of stressed syllables appear to be correlated with stress (Ladefoged, Draper, and Whitteridge, 1958).

In connected speech, muscular activity is not so regular; however, there are usually a number of bursts of increased activity. These bursts do not stand in a one-to-one relationship to syllables. Stetson (1951) had claimed that there is an identifiable "chest pulse" for each syllable; recent electromyographic studies have demonstrated, however, that there is no evidence for such chest pulses. Ladefoged, Draper, and Whitteridge (1958) showed that sometimes a single increase in tension spans a group of articulations including two vowels separated by a consonant closure (in words like *pity* and *around*); and sometimes there are two separate bursts of activity in what is normally regarded as a single syllable (in words like *sport* and *stay*). However, in connected speech the bursts of intercostal activity correlate fairly well with occurrences of the principal stresses of the utterances.

Inferential evidence against the necessary presence of chest pulses as physiological correlates of syllabicity and stress is provided by the fact that quite normal syllabification patterns occur in the speech of some patients with essentially complete paralysis of the respiratory musculature who use an iron lung for respiration (Peterson, 1956). If the patients have retained relatively normal control of the vocal system, they can produce highly inflectional speech with what appear to be entirely normal syllable patterns within each phrase. Peterson's subjects could only speak during the exhaust cycle of the respirator, and they had to time their speech accordingly. They were characteristically unable to produce loud voice without the aid of some special technique to increase the breath pressures during phonation, but with this limitation their stress patterns were apparently normal.

Electromyographic studies and experimental investigations of changes in subglottal pressure have not yet advanced to the point where it would be possible to establish the physiological correlates of different degrees of stress. It is likewise not yet certain whether subglottal activity differentiates between stress and emphasis. Ladefoged (1968, quoted in Lieberman, 1968), has reported that a peak in the subglottal pressure function occurs regularly when a speaker wishes to emphasize part of an utterance. Lieberman (1968) found this to be, indeed, the case for short sentences; however, when speakers were instructed to emphasize several noncontiguous words in a longer sentence, they did not consistently produce a peak in the subglottal air pressure function for each emphasized word. The words were still perceived as emphasized: evidently, phonetic prominence was then produced by other means (cf. Section 4.4).

4.2. Acoustic manifestation of stress

There is no one-to-one correspondence between stress and any single acoustic parameter. Thus, there is also no automatic way to identify stressed syllables. It was found in the previous section that subglottal pressure peaks could be associated with sentence stress and with emphasis; however, stress functions linguistically also at the level of words, and neither electromyography nor measurements of subglottal pressure yield unambiguous evidence for the location of stress within word-level units (unless the word receives sentence stress or emphasis).

There is nevertheless some evidence that stress is judged in terms of effort. If all other factors are kept constant, greater effort will produce a higher degree of stress. It was seen earlier that the force exerted by respiratory muscles is directly transmitted to the air inside the lungs, and this effort is reflected in subglottal pressure. In this section, I should like to consider first the relationship between subglottal pressure and sound pressure, and then the intensity and amplitude of sound waves.

In preparing the following description, I have consulted various handbooks dealing with acoustics (Fletcher, 1953; Kinsler and Frey, 1950; Denes and Pinson, 1963).

The subglottal pressure in the lungs produces an airstream that passes through the glottis with a volume velocity that is proportional to the subglottal pressure. In the production of voiced sounds, the airstream sets the vocal folds in vibration, and the kinetic energy of the airflow is transduced into acoustic energy. Acoustic energy is related to effective sound pressure (amount of force acting over a unit area of surface). As a first approximation, peak subglottal pressure is proportional to the 0.6 power of the peak effective sound pressure (Ladefoged and McKinney, 1963).

The unit of pressure used in acoustic measurements is the dyne per square centimeter. Normal atmospheric pressure is equal to about one million dynes per square centimeter. The pressures that move air particles are very small. The smallest pressure variation sufficient to produce an audible sound wave is equal to about 0.0002 dynes per square centimeter. This value is often taken as reference pressure.

A frequently used unit of work and energy is the erg. One erg is the amount of work done when a force of one dyne displaces an object by one centimeter. Power is the amount of work done in a given time; its unit is the erg per second. The power transmitted along the sound wave through an area of one square centimeter at right angles to the direction of propagation is called the *intensity* of the sound wave (Fletcher, 1934).

The intensity level of a sound of intensity I is defined by the formula

$$n = 10 \log (I/I_0)$$

where n is its intensity level in *decibels* (dB) and I_0 is some reference intensity. Frequently, the reference intensity is 10^{-16} watts per square centimeter, which is near the level of a just audible sound.

Decibels are not fixed units, but units of a logarithmic scale. The decibel refers to a certain intensity ratio; the decibel equivalent of a particular intensity ratio is ten times the logarithm to the base 10 of that ratio. The average intensity of speech is about 60 decibels relative to 10^{-16} watts per square centimeter, measured at a distance of one meter from the lips.

Sound intensity is proportional to the square of the pressure variations of the sound wave. Therefore, the decibel equivalent of a particular pressure ratio is 20 times the logarithm to the base 10 of that ratio.

Another property of sound waves is *amplitude*. If a particle (such as an air molecule) is set in vibratory motion, it oscillates back and forth between two positions that mark the extreme limits of its motion. The maximum displacement of the particle from its rest position is called the amplitude of the vibration. The amplitude of a wave does not depend on the frequency of the wave; intensity, however, does. If the frequency of oscillation of a particle of air is doubled, the particle must travel twice as long a distance in the same length of time. Its velocity must then be twice as great; since the average kinetic energy varies with the average square of the velocity, energy will be four times as great. Similarly, if the amplitude of vibration is doubled, the particle must likewise travel twice the distance in the same time, its velocity will be doubled, and the kinetic energy will be four times as great. The intensity of a sound wave thus is proportional to the square of the amplitude times the square of the frequency.

There are various other ways of looking at the energy expended in speech production. If one integrates the area under the instantaneous power curve, one obtains the total energy represented by the wave. In a continuous recording of integrated speech power, some time constant of integration is required, so that one may obtain, for example, a continuous trace of average speech power as a function of time. A reasonable time constant (i.e., integrating time) would be of the order of the fundamental voice period (such as 0.01 sec), since we may assume that the physiological effort employed in the production of a sustained vowel is essentially constant, and that power variations within the fundamental period do not reflect changes in vocal effort and therefore may be eliminated.

The concepts of amplitude, sound pressure, power, energy, and intensity are all related; all of them are involved in the description of the acoustic correlates of respiratory effort. The terms are often employed rather imprecisely. I believe no great harm is done thereby, as long as the terms are used to refer to qualitative and relative differences.

4.3. The perception of loudness and the perception of stress

Reference has been made already to the smallest amount of pressure that produces an audible sound (approximately 0.0002 dynes/cm^2). In fact, the threshold of audibility varies a great deal with individuals and may vary for the same person under different conditions. The sensitivity of the ear differs a great deal in the different frequency regions. The study of hearing is an extensive field of research in itself; in this book, it will be possible to present only the minimum amount of information necessary for the comprehension of the problems connected with the perception of stress. The following description owes much to Fletcher (1953) and Licklider (1951).

The intensity at which a sound is just distinguishable from silence is called the absolute threshold of the sound. If threshold observations are made with pure tones, the sensitivity of the ear can be probed over the whole range of audible frequencies. At the lowest frequencies, a much greater intensity is required for a sound to be audible than at higher frequencies. The ear is most sensitive to frequencies between 1,000 and 6,000 Hz; at higher frequencies, the sensitivity decreases until at about 15,000 Hz it has again reached a minimum. If the sensitivity of the ear at the frequency at which hearing is most acute is taken as reference (and the intensity of the just-noticeable sound is assigned a value of zero decibels at that frequency), then a just-audible tone at a frequency of 100 Hz must have an intensity that is 40 decibels higher. At a frequency of 10,000 Hz, a tone must be about 10 decibels more intense than the reference intensity to be just audible.

Intensity is a physical characteristic of sound. Loudness is the subjective property of a sound that is most directly related to intensity. Loudness also depends, however, upon the fundamental frequency and the spectral characteristics of the sound as well as on its duration. Each of these relationships will be briefly considered here.

The different sensitivity of the ear to different frequencies forms the basis of the dependence of loudness upon frequency. Of two sounds of equal intensity but of different frequency, one may be subjectively louder than the other if it falls into a frequency range at which the ear is more sensitive. To compare the loudness levels of different sounds, the so-called phon scale was established (Fletcher, 1953). The loudness level of a given tone is defined as the intensity (measured in decibels) of a 1,000-Hz tone that sounds equal in loudness to the given tone. The unit of loudness level is named the phon. A pure tone of 1,000 Hz, at an intensity level of 40 decibels, has a loudness level of 40 phons.

The phon scale of loudness level can be used to rank sensations in order of increasing magnitude; however, the phon scale does not express numerical relations between the measured sensations. A numerical scale of loudness is the sone scale (Fletcher and Munson, 1933; Stevens, 1936). Listeners judge a sound having a loudness of two sones to be twice as loud as a one-sone sound. The sone is the unit of loudness on this numerical scale; a loudness of one sone has been arbitrarily assigned to a 1,000 Hz tone at an intensity level of 40 decibels above threshold, heard with both ears. The sensation of loudness is not directly proportional to loudness level.

The dependence of the loudness of a complex sound upon its spectral characteristics results from the fact that the loudness of complex tones is equal to the sum of the loudnesses of the several components (Howes, 1950).

In order to study the effect of stimulus duration upon perceived loudness, it is necessary to use bursts of noise as stimuli, since at very short durations frequencies become distorted. The problem was first investigated by Miller (1948); Miller's study was replicated and expanded by Small, Brandt, and Cox (1962). Miller found that a short burst of noise must be more intense in order to be equal in effectiveness to a longer noise. Thus, the threshold of hearing is lowered by increasing the duration of the noise up to durations at least as long as one second. The loudness of an intense noise, however, depends upon its duration up to durations of only 65 msec. Judgments of the slowest rate of decay of a noise that sounded indistinguishable from an abrupt termination also led to the concept of a critical time of approximately 65 msec for the sensation to decay to threshold from any steady magnitude of stimulation.

Miller infers from these data that the auditory system acts as if the growth and decay periods of the noise perception depended upon differences in latencies among the various neural paths in transmitting the cochlear activity to the higher centers of the brain. According to this hypothesis, the activity in the slowest pathways arrives at the higher center 65 msec after the activity of the fastest pathways.

Small, Brandt, and Cox (1962) found that above a critical duration, loudness was independent of duration, but below it, for each decade decrease in duration, the level of the short burst of noise had to be increased about 12.5 dB, independent of the level at which the standard burst was presented. The critical duration established in this study was somewhat smaller than that found by Miller: the point above which loudness became independent of duration was approximately 50 msec for a sensation level of 10 dB, decreasing to 15 msec at 60 dB sensation level.

The differential threshold of intensity, i.e., the just-noticeable difference in intensity, remains to be discussed. It has been shown (Riesz, 1928) that it is a function of the frequency and the intensity of the stimulus used as reference. According to Riesz, the minimum intensity change normal listeners can detect for 1,000 Hz at 30 dB sensation level of the reference tone is approximately 1 dB. At levels of 60 or 70 dB above threshold, an increment of less than 0.5 dB is detectable. As a function of frequency, the differential threshold of intensity is smallest at about 2,500 Hz, the minimum being more sharply defined at low sound intensities than it is at high sound intensities. The frequency at which the ear is most sensitive to intensity differences corresponds to the region of the greatest absolute sensitivity of the ear. Riesz calculated that at about 1,300 Hz the ear can distinguish 370 separate tones between the threshold of hearing and the threshold of feeling.

The fundamental frequency of phonation is, as a rule, much lower than the region between 1,300 and 2,500 Hz; however, this region approximates that of the second formant, which carries a great deal of information about speech.

The method used by Riesz was that of beating tones. The source of sound was a special moving-coil telephone receiver actuated by alternating currents from vacuum-tube oscillators. No attempt was made to approximate any vowellike sound. The stimuli used by Flanagan (1957a) were much closer to real speech: different versions of the synthetic vowel [æ], transduced by headphones at a level of approximately 70 dB relative to 0.0002 dyne/cm². Flanagan studied experimentally the just-discriminable change in the amplitude of the second formant of this synthetic vowel sound. Two patterns of fundamental frequency inflection were examined: 120 Hz monotone and linear inflection from 95 to 105 Hz. The results indicated that a change of 3 dB in the amplitude of the second formant was detected approximately 50% of the time for both inflectional patterns. In another study, Flanagan found that the difference limen for overall amplitude for a synthetic vowel was approximately ±1 dB (Flanagan, 1957b).

All these studies have one procedural aspect in common: the stimuli used in the experiments are typical psychophysical stimuli—pure tones and noises—and the perceptual judgments reveal more about the capacities of the organs of perception than about the function of the perceived differences in speech. In the perception of loudness it becomes especially clear that when loudness judgments are made with reference to real speech, the results differ a great deal from judgments made with reference to psychoacoustic stimuli.

I became acutely aware of the problem during a search for acoustic correlates of stress in American English (Lehiste and Peterson, 1959). During this study, we tried to correlate observed differences in vowel amplitude with the perception of stress. It is well known (Black, 1949; Fairbanks, House, and Stevens, 1950) that phonetic changes normally affect vowel amplitudes. Since the human vocal tract is a variable acoustical tube, with a variable radiating orifice, one should not expect to obtain the same pressure or power outputs for identical physiological input energies. Changes of amplitude of the sound wave may be caused by two major factors: first, if the phonetic quality of the vowel is held constant, a change in the amount of input power used to produce the sound may result in a change in output; second, if input energy is kept constant, a change in the phonetic quality of the vowel may result in a change in the output amplitude. The question is now whether these changes in output amplitude are perceived as differences in loudness or differences in stress, or whether they are perceived at all.

As a first step in the study, we recorded a series of vowels while the speaker tried to maintain equal effort. The tapes were then reproduced and the amplitude values were read from a VU meter. Differences between the average amplitudes of high vowels (such as /i/ and /u/) and low vowels (such as /a/) were of the order of 5 dB when the speaker used subjectively constant effort.

In listening casually to the vowels recorded with subjectively equal effort, they appeared to be equally loud. This observation was surprising, since from what is known about the loudness of sinusoidal complexes, it seems very improbable that the vowels would appear equally loud if judged on that basis (Howes, 1950). As was mentioned earlier, for synthetic vowels the just-discriminable change in the amplitude of the second formant is approximately 3 dB, and the difference limen for their overall amplitude is approximately ± 1 dB. Thus, the differences in intensity should result in perceived differences in loudness, if indeed the listener is basing his judgment on the same physical differences in the perception of psychoacoustic stimuli and in the perception of normal speech.

The casual observation of the equal loudness of the vowels was checked in the following manner. Another series of lists of randomized vowels was recorded; this time the speaker watched a VU meter in the recording room and produced all vowels at the same VU level. Some vowels, notably /i/ and /u/, required considerably greater effort than others. A tape was then prepared in which various vowels produced with equal effort were mixed at random with vowels produced with unequal effort but equal in pressure level as measured by the VU meter. The vowels were arranged in random pairs and were presented to listeners, who were asked to judge the relative loudness of the two paired vowels. The listeners were specifically asked to judge the relative *loudness* of the vowels rather than their relative stress or accentuation. Almost invariably, the listeners identified the vowels that were produced with a greater amount of effort (such as /i/ and /u/ recorded at zero VU) as louder than vowels having greater amplitude but produced with normal effort (such as /a/ and /ɔ/ in the first set of recordings).

One way to explain this phenomenon would be to assume that the listeners were not reacting to the actual intensity differences but were in fact responding to differences in effort, whatever the cues may have been that were present in the sound waves to indicate the relative amount of effort the speaker had used in producing the vowels. Likewise, the speakers identified vowels as being equally loud when they were produced with equal effort, regardless of physical intensity differences that were in fact present. This suggests that the listeners may associate a certain intrinsic relative amplitude (or perhaps average power) with each vowel spectrum, and apply a corresponding "correction factor" to the incoming signal. Assuming that duration and fundamental voice frequency are held constant, this procedure would enable a listener to identify a stressed syllable, even if the average or peak power of that syllable were less than that of an adjacent unstressed syllable containing a more open vowel.

The experiments just summarized provide additional evidence for the so-called motor theory of speech production (Liberman et al., 1963).

Stress perception thus seems to be quite different from the perception of loudness. It presupposes a speech setting and also, if the notion of "correction factors" has some validity, a certain amount of learning. Daniel Jones (1940) is the only phonetician who explicitly states that stress perception also involves knowledge of the language in which the utterance is spoken. Jones distinguishes between stress and prominence. According to Jones, the prominence of a syllable is its general degree of distinctness, this being the combined effect of the timbre, length, stress, and (if voiced) intonation of the syllabic sound. The term *stress* refers only to the degree of force of utterance; it is independent of length and intonation, although it may be combined with these. Prominence is a perceptual quantity that may be decreased or increased by means of any of the sound attributes (length, stress, pitch, timbre); stress is an articulatory gesture. Jones seems to anticipate the motor theory of speech perception when he suggests that a person familiar with a language does not perceive the sounds objectively from the physical stimulus, but perceives them in a subjective way: the sounds he hears call up to his mind the manner of making them, and by means of immediate "inner speech," he knows where the stress is.

Although Jones distinguishes between stress and prominence, he does not make it clear which of them has linguistic function, or whether they may have different linguistic functions. It would perhaps be advisable to use the term *stress* to refer to prominence produced by means of respiratory effort (the "expiratory accent" of older phoneticians), and to employ the term *accent* when prominence is achieved by other phonetic means in place of or in addition to respiratory effort. I shall continue to use the term *stress* to refer to linguistically significant prominence; however, I shall make clear in instances where it is relevant which of the phonetic factors is involved in producing this prominence.

4.4. Phonetic correlates of stress

4.4.1. Intrinsic intensity of speech sounds

As was mentioned earlier, phonetic changes normally affect vowel amplitudes. The intensity of a vowel thus can serve as a cue for the presence of stress only when two vowels of identical spectral structure are being compared. The intrinsic intensity of a vowel is its intensity considered in relation to its phonetic quality. Table 4.1 gives an idea of the differences in the intrinsic intensities of syllable nuclei in American English.

As a rough test of the afore-mentioned influence of vowel quality upon stress in English, I performed the following brief

Table 4.1. Intrinsic Intensity of Syllable Nuclei*

Syllable nucleus	Average values for one speaker†	Averages for each vowel‡
i	80.1	75.1
ɪ	81.3	78.1
eɪ	81.1	78.6
ɛ	83.4	79.3
æ	83.0	79.4
ə	84.5	79.7
a	85.7	80.2
ɔ	85.6	80.6
oᵁ	83.5	79.7
ʊ	83.3	78.4
u	80.4	78.2
aʊ	84.4	80.1
aɪ	82.5	80.2
ɔɪ	84.1	80.9
ɝ	81.4	79.0
Average for all vowels	83.0	79.0

* After Lehiste and Peterson, 1959.
† VU meter readings for sustained vowels relative to 0.0002 dyne/cm².
‡ Produced in 1,263 monosyllables.

experiment (Lehiste and Peterson, 1959). A series of words that distinguish between the two categories of noun and verb by means of contrastive stress placement (such as DIgest-diGEST) were recorded by a native speaker. The words were produced within the sentence frame 'Say the word . . . again'; an attempt was made to use the same degree of effort in the production of each test word. The words were then analyzed spectrographically, and the differences between the amplitudes of the syllable nuclei were noted. The only pair in which vowel quality remained fairly constant in both productions was PERvert–perVERT; the amplitude difference between the stressed and unstressed syllable in this word pair was approximately 2 dB. This was considered to reflect the difference in input energy. It should also be an audible difference considering that the just-discriminable difference is approximately 1 dB. Figure 4.1 contains broad-band spectrograms, narrow-band spectrograms, and continuous-amplitude displays of this word pair and the pair INcline–inCLINE. The difference in amplitude for the two syllables of INcline is approximately zero dB; according to Table 4.1, the intrinsic amplitude of [ɪ] is 78.1 and that of [aɪ] 80.2 decibels in monosyllabic test words produced in the same frame by the same speakers. If the correction factor of approximately 2 dB is applied, the difference between the stressed and unstressed syllables of INcline equals that observed in the production of PERvert.

Intrinsic intensities have been established for a number of other languages. Fónagy (1966) reports values for Hungarian as shown in Table 4.2. There is a considerable phonetic difference between short and long vowels in Hungarian. The long vowels have tense and close articulation, while short vowels are relatively more lax and open. Short /a/ is somewhat raised and labialized. This explains why in all cases except for the /a/–/a:/ pair, the short vowels have greater intrinsic intensities than the long vowels. The 12 dB range is rather large, compared to the 4 to 5 dB range established for American English; Fónagy suggests that this may be due to

Figure 4.1. Broad-band spectrograms, continuous amplitude displays, and narrow-band spectrograms of the four words perVERT, PERvert, inCLINE, and INcline, embedded in the carrier sentence "Say the word . . . again." The frequency scales for the spectrograms are linear up to 3,600 Hz; the amplitude scale is nonlinear

Table 4.2. Intensities of Vowels in Disyllabic Hungarian Words (in dB relative to /a:/)*

Short vowels		Long vowels	
/i/	−7.2	/i:/	−9.7
/y/	−9.0	/y:/	−10.2
/u/	−10.6	/u:/	−12.3
/e/	−1.3	/e:/	−3.6
/ɸ/	−3.2	/ɸ:/	−5.8
/o/	−5.1	/o:/	−7.2
/a/	−2.4	/a:/	0.0

* After Fónagy, 1966.

the careful articulation of the test words. Tentative measurements based on a smaller number of carelessly articulated tokens indicated a reduction in range to 6 to 7 dB.

The concept of intrinsic intensity is, of course, much older than the quoted studies, and was already known to such phoneticians as Sievers (1893) and Rousselot (1924).

Thus, the intrinsic intensity of vowels due to their phonetic quality is one factor that must be taken into consideration in the interpretation of intensity data. Another factor is the interaction between fundamental frequency and formant frequency. The relative independence of the glottal and supraglottal effects makes possible the mathematical description of speech sounds by specifying the source function and the filter function, which together determine the system function (Fant, 1960). Such a specification indicates that the glottal output serves to excite a resonating system whose characteristics determine the various spectra associated with vowels. The spacing of the harmonics generated at the glottis is independent of the center frequencies of the resonances of the vocal tract. If the articulatory configuration of the vocal tract remains fixed and the fundamental frequency of the voice is changed, extensive changes in overall level will occur; the amplitude will increase if a harmonic coincides with the frequency of one of the lower formants, especially the first formant (since most of the energy of the vowel is contained in the first formant).

This "optimal vocal frequency" was studied with synthetic vowels by House (1959), who found that the overall intensity of synthetic vowels could fluctuate by as much as 5 to 6 dB, depending on whether harmonic frequency coincided with the first formant.

The interaction of harmonic frequency and formant frequency was studied in real speech by Peterson and McKinney (1961) and Ladefoged and McKinney (1963). In these studies, words were spoken with a long falling pitch while the speaker maintained subjectively equal effort. The power-level oscillogram was observed in some cases to have one to four rather prominent peaks, although the words were phonated evenly. It was found that these peaks occurred at just the times when the harmonic frequencies passed through formant center frequencies. The differences in amplitude between the maxima and minima of the intensity curve were of the order of several decibels. Ladefoged and McKinney, who also recorded subglottal pressure while the words were produced, noted that these words had only one peak of subglottal pressure and apparently only one peak of loudness. Since auditory perception operates with a comparatively long time constant in loudness judgments (Miller, 1948; Small, Brandt, and Cox, 1962), these fluctuations in output intensity may probably be considered irrelevant in the perception of stress. In the practical problem of intensity measurement, it is advisable to use a time constant (of the order of 20 centiseconds) in the smoothing circuit that will eliminate short-term fluctuations in the intensity curve.

There is a further factor that makes the interpretation of intensity curves in terms of stress extremely difficult, and this is the difference in intensity between a vowel target and the transitions from and to the adjacent consonants. The intensity of the vocalic portion of a syllable nucleus depends on its formant structure; however, the formant structure does not remain constant throughout the vowel, the initial and terminal frequencies of the formants being determined by the preceding and following consonant. For example, in sequences involving a high vowel flanked by dental/alveolar consonants, the intensity of the syllable nucleus is greater during the transitions than during the target portion of the vowel.

4.4.2. The role of fundamental frequency, intensity, and duration in the perception of stress One problem in interpreting the physiological and acoustic correlates of stress is the ambiguous role of intensity in the perception of stress. While there is a direct link between increases in respiratory effort, subglottal pressure, and the amplitude of the sound wave, intensity seems to provide a rather weak cue for the perception of stress. One reason for this lack of a more direct relationship between intensity and stress is the fact, discussed earlier, that output intensity changes with the articulatory configuration of the vocal tract. Another is provided by the fact that subglottal pressure is also one of the physiological factors that control the rate of vocal fold vibration. Thus, stress is intimately connected with frequency. Unless an adjustment is provided in the tension of the vocal folds, increased subglottal pressure results automatically in an increased rate of vocal fold vibration. Therefore, in many languages, higher fundamental frequency provides a strong cue for the presence of stress.

While increase in respiratory effort provides an obvious physiological cause for increases in intensity and increases in the rate of vocal fold vibration, no such reason is apparent for a frequent third phonetic correlate of stressedness: greater duration. There are many languages in which a stressed syllable is longer than an unstressed one. This appears to be a language-determined phenomenon; the presumed generality of the feature, sometimes implied in the literature, may be due to the fact that duration is indeed a stress cue in many Western European languages that have been subjected to instrumental phonetic study.

The relative importance of intensity, fundamental frequency, and duration in the perception of stress have been studied experimentally in several languages, including English (Fry, 1955, 1958; Bolinger, 1958; Morton and Jassem, 1965), Polish (Jassem, Morton, and Steffen-Batóg, 1968), French

(Rigault, 1962), Swedish (Westin, Buddenhagen, and Obrecht, 1966), and Serbo-Croatian (Rehder, 1968). I shall review briefly the findings reported in these studies in the order in which the languages were just presented.

In his classic study of 1955, Fry used the Haskins Laboratories' Pattern-Playback synthesizer (Cooper, Liberman, and Borst, 1951) to produce test words of the type *object, digest, permit,* in which he varied the duration and intensity of both syllables in a systematic fashion. The values chosen for intensity were as follows: vowel 1/vowel 2, equal; vowel 1, +5 dB, +10 dB, −5 dB, −10 dB. Five duration ratios between the two syllables were selected; these values were adapted somewhat to the observed durations of the two syllables in actual productions of the words. For example, for the word *permit* the ratios were 0.50, 0.75, 1.00, 1.50, and 2.00; for the word *contract*, 0.20, 0.40, 0.60, 0.80, 1.00.

The listening test was administered to 100 subjects. In words in which duration and intensity were operating in the same direction, there was excellent agreement between the subjects: when the vowel was long and of high intensity, listeners agreed that the vowel was strongly stressed; when it was short and of low intensity, it was judged as weakly stressed. At other points in the range, the degree of agreement varied from word to word, but several items for each word divided the listeners about equally.

When the effects of duration and intensity were studied separately, it became clear that duration provided the overriding cue. When intensity was kept constant, increasing duration ratio (V1/V2) increased the "noun" judgments (i.e., the identification of the first syllable as stressed) by 70%. The whole range of intensity change produced an increase of only 29% in the number of "noun" judgments.

In the study published in 1958, Fry tested three parameters—intensity, duration, and fundamental frequency—as cues for the perception of stress. The stimuli were likewise produced on the Pattern-Playback synthesizer; in addition, the fundamental frequency of one word pair (*subject*) was systematically manipulated by means of a device in which hand-painted spectrograms were used to control the synthesizer action of an 18-channel vocoder (Borst and Cooper, 1957). In tests with this word pair, two physical dimensions were explored at the same time; the duration ratios already used with *subject* were combined with step-changes of frequency ranging from 5 to 90 Hz. The intensity ratio was kept constant at equal intensity for both vowels.

The results of the 1955 study were confirmed for duration and intensity. However, change in fundamental frequency differed from change of duration and intensity in that it tended to produce an all-or-none effect: the magnitude of the frequency change seemed to be relatively unimportant, whereas the fact that a frequency change had taken place appeared to be all-important. The experiments with a step-change in frequency showed that a higher syllable was more likely to be perceived as stressed. Additional experiments with more complex patterns of fundamental frequency change suggested that sentence intonation is an overriding factor in determining the perception of stress, and that in this sense the fundamental frequency cue may outweigh the duration cue.

Fry (1965) has also studied the effect of a fourth cue, the phonetic value of the vowel, in the perception of stress. In a series of synthetic productions of the word pairs comprising the nouns and verbs *object*, *contrast*, and *digest*, Fry changed systematically the first and second formant frequencies of the vowels. The fundamental frequency of the periodic sounds was kept constant at 120 Hz. The overall intensity of syllables was regulated so that the maximum intensity in the two syllables of a test word was equal; a constant difference between formant 1 and formant 2 was maintained throughout. Variations in vowel duration ratio were introduced in the same stimuli in order to provide a means of estimating the weight to be assigned to the changes in formant structure. While Fry admits that it is very difficult to compare the changes in duration ratio and in formant positions, the results of listening tests indicated that in the conditions of this experiment, the weight of the duration cue was considerably greater than that of the formant structure cue. It appeared that the formant structure cue for stress may even have been less effective than the intensity cue.

Over a number of years, Bolinger performed a series of experiments using both natural and artificial speech to study the phonetic and linguistic nature of stress (summarized in Bolinger, 1958). He reached the conclusion that the primary cue of what is usually termed stress in the utterance is pitch prominence. Bolinger regarded duration as a covariable with pitch, but rejected the notion that intensity plays a crucial role. Bolinger suggested that at the level of utterances it is better to speak of pitch accent than of stress; the term *stress* should be relegated to the domain of word stress. In the latter domain, one possible kind of phonemic stress is potential for pitch accent. Bolinger seems to have ignored differences in intrinsic intensity in evaluating his experimental results. It is possible that some of his results would lend themselves to reinterpretation if intrinsic intensity differences are taken into account.

Morton and Jassem (1965) used synthetic nonsense syllables of the form /sisi/, /sɔsɔ/ and /sasa/, produced on PAT, a parametric speech synthesizer (Lawrence, 1953). The stimuli were expressly constructed to have the same vowels in both syllables in order to avoid the problem of different intrinsic intensities. The parameters of fundamental frequency, intensity, and duration were varied systematically. English listeners showed a high degree of consistency in their responses. Variations in fundamental frequency produced far greater effects than variations in either intensity or duration; a syllable was marked stressed if it was different from the "context" fundamental, and a raised fundamental was more efficient than a lowered one. In general, the more intense and longer syllables were more likely to be marked as stressed. The results of Morton and Jassem confirm the "all-or-none" effect of fundamental frequency changes already observed by Fry; changes of 25 and 58 % in the fundamental frequency (i.e., step-ups from 120 Hz to 151 or 190 Hz, or step-downs from 120 Hz to 96 or 76 Hz) were equally effective in producing stress judgments.

Jassem, Morton, and Steffen-Batóg (1968) presented almost exactly the same stimuli to Polish listeners. A comparison of the behavior of the two different groups of subjects revealed both similarities and differences. A striking similarity was the strong effect, in both languages, of fundamental frequency variations. Interestingly enough, variations in duration were more effective with Polish than with English listeners. Intensity was ineffective until a difference of 6 dB was reached; however, the effect of this difference could be outweighed by differences in duration. In earlier studies, Jassem (1959) had concluded from his measurements of the same three acoustic parameters that Polish stress is mainly signaled by fundamental frequency.

Rigault (1962), also using synthetic speech produced with PAT, synthesized the word *papa* and the phrase *'Qu'est-ce que vous faites?'*. Systematic variations of the three parameters—frequency, intensity, and duration—were produced, and the test tapes were presented to French listeners. The results showed again that frequency was by far the most important physical correlate of perceived stress. The relative importance of duration and intensity seemed to be approximately the same. When frequency was kept constant, the word *papa* was judged to have been stressed on the initial syllable 75% of the time if the first syllable had both high intensity and long duration. When the first syllable had high intensity but short duration, it was judged as stressed in 35% of cases; weak intensity and long duration produced judgments of stressedness on the first syllable in 40% of the cases. In all these items, the second syllable had long duration and medium intensity.

Westin, Buddenhagen, and Obrecht (1966) studied the relative importance of frequency, duration, and intensity as cues for syllabic prominence in Southern Swedish. Using tape-splicing techniques, they produced combinations of two versions of *hälsa på* (meaning 'to visit' or 'to greet', depending on accent) in which the first and last syllable had fundamental frequencies of either 122 or 144 Hz, durations of either 195 or 300 msec, and either high or low intensity, the difference being 6 dB. Listening tests were administered to speakers of Swedish in Lund. Analysis of the results showed again that frequency provided the primary cue for identifications. Significantly, the frequency of the first syllable was the more potent cue, over-riding opposing cues of pitch, quantity, and intensity on the final syllable. The authors concluded that perception followed primarily the first syllable, that subjects made their identifica-tions on the basis of the fundamental frequency of the first syllable, and that they could not be dissuaded in their identifi-cations by contradictory information present in the final syllable. It could not be established with certainty which of the two remaining cues, quantity or intensity, was the more important.

The results obtained for Swedish look similar to those presented earlier with reference to English, French, and Polish. It should be kept in mind, though, that Swedish is presumed to have a tonal accent anyway; therefore the prevalence of the fundamental frequency cue in stress judgments is not very surprising and probably should be interpreted differently than in the case of languages without contrastive tone. The im-portance of the first syllable in the perception of the accent is surprising, however, since in many descriptions of the pho-nology of Swedish the domain of the accentual patterns is considered to be a word (Elert, 1964; but cf. Efremova, Fintoft, and Ormestad, 1965, for similar results in Norwegian).

Rehder (1968) attempted to establish the relative importance of fundamental frequency and intensity as distinctive com-ponents of Serbo-Croatian accents by using what he calls "purposeful destruction" and "purposeful construction" of the signals. A vocoder was used for manipulating frequency, and a specially built intensity compressor for manipulating intensity. Selected minimal accentual pairs, produced by native informants, were processed and re-recorded under the following conditions: (a) fundamental frequency unchanged, intensity leveled by means of the intensity compressor; (b) intensity unchanged, frequency monotonized at 155 Hz by means of the vocoder; (c) both parameters leveled at the same time in the manner described above. Listening tests indicated that fundamental frequency was the decisive parameter in identification. The final identification scores might be quoted. Under condition (a) (original frequency, leveled intensity), the identifications were 95.4% correct; under condition (b) (original intensity, fundamental frequency monotonous at 155 Hz), 53.6%; under condition (c) (both cues eliminated), 47.8%.

In all these experiments the time dimension was not affected and quantity relationships remained unchanged. An interesting perceptual phenomenon emerged during the study: the syllable nuclei with long rising accents made a perceptually longer impression after being processed through the vocoder than the syllable nuclei with long falling accents. These subjective length differences were present under condition (b) but not under condition (c). Rehder speculates that they might have been due to intensity differences in the last third of the accented long syllable nuclei. The originally rising syllable nuclei presumably had greater intensity during the last third of their duration than originally falling syllable nuclei; this greater intensity might have been perceived as additional length in the case of originally long rising syllable nuclei. These instrumentally caused perceptual artifacts were not distinctive, as may be seen from the reported identification scores; they may nevertheless explain the slightly higher (although nondistinctively so) scores achieved under condition (b) as compared to condition (c).

In summary, it appears that in all studies fundamental frequency provided relatively stronger cues for the presence of stress than did intensity. Duration also appeared to play a larger role than intensity; it should be kept in mind, however, that the languages in which the relative importance of the prosodic parameters was studied included only two languages in which duration is contrastive. In experiments with Serbo-Croatian, the durational dimension of the test words remained unchanged. In Swedish, the results were inconclusive with respect to the relative importance of duration and intensity in the perception of stress.

4.4.3. Suprasegmental correlates of stress All the studies reviewed up to now have been devoted to establishing the perceptual significance of various phonetic cues incorporated into listening tests in which the task has been to identify the stressed syllable. The problem of stress may be looked at from another point of view: it may be assumed that the presence of stress is given on a particular syllable, and the phonetic correlates of stress may then be established through a study of the phonetic characteristics of that syllable. The majority of phonetic studies of stress have in fact followed this method. Some of the phonetic correlates of stress will be briefly reviewed here.

Lieberman (1960) studied the acoustic correlates of stress in American English, analyzing 25 verb-noun pairs (of the type CONflict–conFLICT), recorded by 16 speakers of American English. He found that the stressed syllable had a higher fundamental frequency than the unstressed syllable of the same utterance in 90% of the cases, a higher peak envelope amplitude in 87% cases, and a longer duration in 66% instances. The stressed syllable, compared with its unstressed counterpart in the other word of the stress pair, had a higher fundamental frequency in 72% of the cases, a higher peak envelope amplitude in 90% cases, and a longer duration in 70% instances.

Lieberman also computed graphically the integrals of the amplitude with respect to time of the stressed and unstressed syllables of the same word and compared them. In 92% of the cases the integral of the stressed syllable was greater. The ratio of the integrals of the stressed to unstressed syllables of each word was also divided by that of the unstressed to stressed syllables of the other stress form. In 99.9% of the cases the resulting ratio was greater than 1. In no case did the stressed syllable have both a lower amplitude and a lower fundamental frequency than the unstressed syllable. Moreover, the stressed syllable in all but two cases had either a greater integral of amplitude with respect to time (over the syllable's duration), or a longer duration than the unstressed syllable of the same utterance, or both.

Lieberman did not introduce a correction factor to account for the differing intrinsic intensities of the vowels; the changes in vowel quality associated with stress versus lack of stress were likewise ignored. The relative value of the cues he discovered cannot, therefore, be accepted as having been established with complete certainty.

The languages in which frequency seems to be the strongest cue of stressedness also include Polish (Jassem, 1959) and French (Rigault, 1962). Jassem claims specifically that Polish stress is melodic or tonal. In addition, Polish stressed vowels tended to be slightly longer than the same vowels in unstressed syllables; additional intensity sometimes accompanied stress, but there was no correlation between phonetic quality and stress.

In languages such as Hungarian, the criterion employed by Lieberman to establish stressedness cannot be used: vowel duration is independently contrastive in every syllable, and if the intrinsic amplitude of the vowels is the same, the integral of amplitude with respect to time over the duration of an unstressed syllable would be greater in all words in which the first (stressed) syllable contains a short vowel and the second (unstressed) syllable contains a long vowel. Fónagy (1966) presents many instances in which an unstressed second syllable of Hungarian words is longer and has both greater intensity and higher frequency than a stressed syllable. Acoustic analysis failed to provide unambiguous cues to stressedness; however, electromyographic studies (Fónagy, 1958) showed that there was a close correspondence between stress and the activity of the internal intercostals. Fónagy considers his results further evidence for the motor theory of speech perception—stress is identified by the listener's interpretation of the speaker's muscular effort—and would in fact like to limit the term *stress* to prominence produced by means of respiratory effort.

In a study of Serbo-Croatian accents (cf. Chapter 3) we studied the features of duration, intensity, and fundamental frequency as they appeared on syllables that were identified as stressed (Lehiste and Ivić, 1963), and we tried to establish what constitutes accentedness. We found that intensity was not a reliable clue; for some speakers, there were regular differences in the intensity patterns of words with rising and falling accents, while for other speakers no systematic patterns could be established. Table 4.3 shows the results of intensity measurements in the speech of 12 informants. Figure 4.2 shows intensity curves and oscillograms of four test words produced by one of the informants whose speech was analyzed in the study. This informant had the closest correlation between fundamental frequency and intensity. In the speech of this informant, words with falling accents regularly had a 7 to 8 dB drop in intensity between the stressed and posttonic syllable; words with rising accents had a second syllable whose intensity was as great or greater than the intensity of the stressed syllable.

It might be assumed that the intensity rise is an automatic concomitant of higher pitch. This was found not to be the case, however, since there were a great number of instances in which fundamental frequency and intensity went their separate ways. An illustration is provided in Figure 4.3, which contains oscillograms, intensity curves, and fundamental frequency curves of two utterances produced by another Serbo-Croatian informant, in whose speech intensity was not correlated with fundamental frequency. The fundamental frequency curves of the words *râda* and *Ráda* show the typical patterns associated with long falling and long rising accents; the intensity curves of the two words are hardly distinguishable, and, especially in the case of the word with the long rising accent, they move in an opposite direction as compared to the fundamental frequency curve.

Let us now return to the question of what constitutes accentedness in Serbo-Croatian. The question appears relatively simple in the case of words with falling accents. In these words, the posttonic syllables always had lower fundamental frequency than the accented syllables, and in the speech of those informants whose speech exhibited a systematic

Table 4.3. Average Difference in Intensity Between the Peak of the Stressed Syllable and the Immediately Following Syllable in Test Words Produced by 12 Speakers (in dB)*

Speaker	˝ ꞉	ˊ ꞉	˝ ꞉ ꞉	ˋ ꞉ ꞉	꞉꞉ ꞉	ˊ ꞉	All Falling Patterns	All Rising Patterns	Probable Significance
D 1	−9.9	+0.3	−8.0	+1.2	−7.4	−2.3	−8.4	−0.3	+
D 2	−9.0	−5.0	−10.7	−2.8	−10.8	−4.1	−10.2	−4.0	?
D 3	−5.2	−2.7	−1.0	+2.2	−6.5	−1.8	−4.2	−0.8	?
D 5	−8.0	−1.3	−2.6	−0.4	−5.0	−2.5	−5.2	−1.4	?
D 6	−8.2			−1.2	−6.3	−2.1	−7.3	−1.1	+
D 7	−4.7	−1.3	−4.5	−1.5	−7.7	−6.7	−5.6	−3.2	−
D 8	−7.6	−2.5	−10.8	−5.2	−7.2	−2.2	−8.5	−3.3	++
E 10	−8.7	−0.8	−4.0	+3.0	−7.8	−5.0	−6.8	−0.9	+
E 11	−5.0	−1.0	−4.2	−3.1	−3.8	−1.7	−4.3	−1.9	−
E 12	−9.2	−3.9	−7.3	−0.2	−7.6	+0.4	−8.0	−1.2	+
E 13	−8.3	−2.4	−4.7	−1.4	−6.9	−0.8	−6.6	−1.5	++
E 14	−5.2	−2.9	−5.7	−1.6	−3.4	−2.2	−4.8	−2.2	−
Average	−7.4	−2.0	−5.8	−0.9	−6.7	−2.6	−6.7	−1.8	?

* After Lehiste and Ivić, 1963.

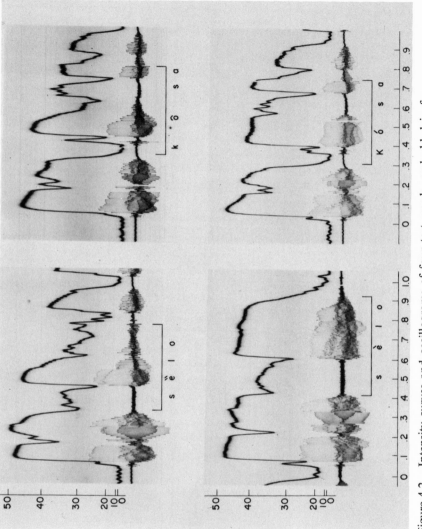

Figure 4.2. Intensity curves and oscillograms of four test words, embedded in frame sentences, as produced by a Serbo-Croatian informant (Lehiste and Ivić, 1963).

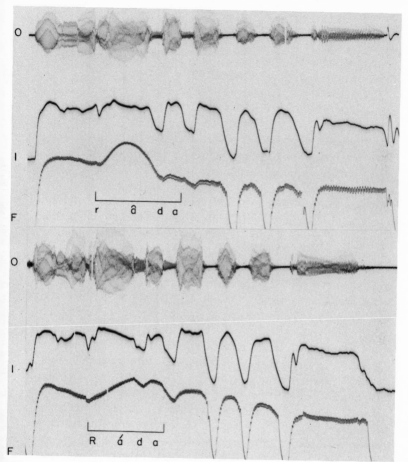

Figure 4.3. Oscillograms, intensity curves, and fundamental frequency curves of two test words, embedded in frame sentences, spoken by a Serbo-Croatian informant (Ivić and Lehiste, 1963).

correlation between frequency and intensity, the posttonic syllables also had lower intensity. However, in words with rising accents the posttonic syllable had either the same or slightly higher fundamental frequency than the syllable usually considered accented. For a number of informants, there was also no difference in the intensity of the two syllables. Thus, we had a case here in which an unstressed syllable could not be distinguished from a stressed syllable on the basis of either fundamental frequency or intensity.

The decisive cue for stressedness appeared in duration. In the version of Standard Serbo-Croatian that formed the basis of our study, there was a ratio of approximately 2:3 between the short and long syllables, whether stressed or unstressed. The same ratio was observed between stressed and unstressed vowels of the same phonemic quantity. This factor was the same, regardless of whether the accent was rising or falling. In words with short rising accents on the first syllable, followed by a short posttonic syllable, both syllables had high pitch and high intensity, but the first syllable nucleus was approximately 1.5 times as long as the second syllable nucleus.

Thus, in many languages, fundamental frequency, combined with intensity, provides the decisive cue; in others, duration is the most dependable correlate of stressedness. There are languages in which unstressed syllables may be regularly longer than stressed syllables. One of these is Estonian. In a study dealing with vowel quantity in words and utterances in Estonian (Lehiste, 1968a), I compared the durations of vowels in words occurring under sentence stress and in subjectively unstressed words. In Estonian, the first syllable of a word is stressed, and odd-numbered syllables ordinarily receive secondary stress. Table 4.4 gives some representative average durations.

In the first word type given in Table 4.4, the ratio between the durations of the vowels in the first and second syllables of 140 stressed words of the given type (95:115) was 0.83; the ratio of the corresponding vowels in 105 unstressed occurrences (59:71) was also 0.83. Although the absolute durations of the vowels in both the first and the second syllables of unstressed words were noticeably decreased, the ratios remained the same (the precise identity of the ratios is probably accidental). I should add that there were many words of this type whose first vowel could not be located on a spectrogram (reduced forms of

Table 4.4. Average Durations of Vowels in Estonian Words of Different Types*

Word type	No. of occurrences	Average duration of vowels in successive syllables (msec)			
		1	2	3	4
Stressed (c)vcv(c)	140	95	115		
Unstressed (c)vcv(c)	105	59	71		
Stressed (c)vvvcv(c)	92	258	102		
Unstressed (c)vvvcv(c)	9	124	60		
Stressed (c)vcvcv(c)	53	83	106	68	
Stressed (c)vcvcvcv(c)	14	79	105	59	96

* After Lehiste, 1968a.

the demonstrative pronoun *seda*), while the unstressed second vowel was clearly identifiable and measurable. The Estonian case implies that the decrease in duration that apparently resulted from lack of stress applied to the word as a whole rather than to a segmental sound, since the basic word shape, as determined by the quantity ratio, did not change. The matter will be discussed further in Chapter 5.

As has been mentioned in preceding chapters, in many languages the occurrence of quantity oppositions or tonal oppositions is conditioned by stress. Conversely, the presence of stress may be inferred from the occurrence of these oppositions in the languages in which such a relationship exists between stress and other suprasegmental features.

4.4.4. Segmental cues to the presence of stress In many languages, there are other cues that signal the difference between stressed and unstressed syllables. One of these is a possible difference in vowel quality. In languages like English, there is a tendency for most vowels in weakly stressed syllables to approach schwa in quality. Stetson (1951) observed that vowel reduction varies along a continuum of stronger and weaker forms, the precise amount of reduction being related to the degree of stress placed on the vowel. With an increase in the rate of production, all vowels in unstressed syllables arrive at the common schwa.

In a study of general American vowels in isolated, stressed, and unstressed positions, Tiffany (1959) found that the acoustical vowel diagram had a tendency to grow smaller from isolated vowel to stressed vowel to unstressed vowel. As the degree of stress diminished, vowels seemed to move toward a neutral, central point of the vowel diagram. Shearme and Holmes (1962) made similar observations in British English. Fant (1962) showed that in Swedish, a decrease in stress, which is in most cases associated with a decrease in the duration of the vowel, shifts the formant pattern of the vowel toward that of the schwa, i.e., approximately 500, 1,500, and 2,500 Hz for the first three formants for a male talker.

In a very informative study of vowel reduction, Lindblom (1963) developed an articulatory model in which articulatory targets are aimed at by the speaker, but the degree of reaching the target depends mainly on the duration of the vowel. The term *target* can be given an explicit definition in terms of the asymptotic values of the first-formant frequencies of a given vowel. A target is independent of consonantal context and duration and can thus be looked upon as an invariant attribute of the vowel. Although a vowel phoneme can be realized in a more or less reduced fashion, the talker's "intention" that underlies the pronunciation of the vowel is always the same, independent of contextual circumstances. On the basis of the "undershoot" that was present in his data, Lindblom concluded that the talker does not adjust the control of his vocal tract at fast rates to compensate for its response delay. Vowel reduction is thus, according to Lindblom's hypothesis, due to timing rather than to a lesser degree of effort in the articulation of unstressed vowels.

Lindblom's theory seems to presuppose that unstressed syllables are progressively shortened, which seems to be the case in English as well as in Swedish, the language that provided Lindblom's test materials. There may nevertheless be differences in quality between stressed and unstressed vowels that cannot be explained either by the schwa hypothesis or by the shortening/undershoot hypothesis.

One such difference is the appearance of a smaller—and different—set of vowels in unstressed position. This phenomenon is very common. Only a few languages need to be quoted to illustrate the fact. For example, in Russian there is a set of five vowel phonemes that occur in stressed position; in unstressed positions, there are three or four contrastive vowels. The vowel reduction rule is clearly language-specific. Its main features are as follows: in posttonic position, the five vowels /ieaou/ are replaced by a set of three vowels (a reduced high front unrounded vowel, a high back rounded vowel, and a reduced mid vowel). In immediately pretonic position and/or word-initial position, four vowels may occur, three of which are phonetically similar to stressed versions of /ieu/; the fourth represents the neutralization of the vowels /a/ and /o/ in a sound that is phonetically close to /a/. In other pretonic positions, the same set of vowels is found as in posttonic positions (Avanesov, 1956). The particular system of neutralization that is found in Russian (especially the merging of /e/ and /i/ in a vowel that is phonetically close to [i] and the merging of /o/ and /a/ in immediately pretonic position in a sound that is phonetically close to [a]) cannot be explained by either the schwa hypothesis or the undershoot hypothesis.

Even without any clear difference in vowel quality, lack of stress may be correlated with the occurrence of a smaller set of vowels. In Estonian, for example, the nine vowels /aeiouõäöü/ occur in the stressed first syllable of a word, whereas only four vowels (the subset /aeiu/) are found in unstressed syllables and as second components of diphthongs. When a compound noun loses its compound character and is phonetically adapted to noncompound word patterns, the vowels /oõäöü/ that may have occurred in the first syllable of the second member of the compound are replaced by /aeiu/ (Lehiste, 1964a). This is a language-specific feature, and probably a late development in Estonian; Finnish, for example, has no such restrictions on the occurrence of its eight vowels, although Finnish has distributional restrictions of a different kind due to vowel harmony.

Further segmental cues to the presence of stress may consist of the occurrence of special consonant allophones in stressed syllables, such as aspirated plosives. There may also be further differences, either allophonic or phonotactic in nature,

between the segmental sounds occurring in stressed and unstressed syllables. Such segmental and distributional clues to
the presence of stress will not be treated further in this essay.

4.5. *The linguistic function of stress*

In the part dealing with the linguistic function of stress, I
should like to consider first the possible differences in stress
type and then the question of stress position. This leads
naturally into the problem of the domain of stress placement,
and thus to the question of differentiating between word stress,
sentence stress, contrastive stress, and emphasis.

4.5.1. Types of stress It is traditional in phonetics to divide
stress into the so-called dynamic or expiratory stress and the
musical or melodic stress. This assumption seems to have
been based on a belief that stress and pitch are independent of
each other—a belief that was current also in the 1940's and
1950's in the United States. An early critic of the traditional
distinction between dynamic and musical stress was Saran
(1907). Saran insisted that the analysis of stress must proceed
from the standpoint of the hearer. The reason that intensity
cannot be considered a factor of stress besides pitch and
duration is, according to Saran, that the increase in breath
force used in producing stressed syllables is a reality for the
speaker but is not felt as such by the hearer. The hearer
perceives only the acoustic effect of increased effort—namely,
loudness. Saran refers to experimental studies of perception
then in progress according to which the sensitivity of the ear
for differences in loudness is much less than that for differences
in duration, whereas it was a fact already well known in
Saran's time that the ear is capable of quite fine frequency
discriminations.

Later phoneticians, such as Schmitt (1924), criticized the
distinction between dynamic and musical stress, but for
different reasons. They assumed that expiratory differences
normally go together with melodic differences, and that,
therefore, a sharp distinction between the two types is
unwarranted.

Phonologists of the Prague school used the term *corrélation dynamique* as one of the forms of *corrélation tonique*. Jakobson (1931), conceding that languages cannot be classified into those having musical accent and those having dynamic accent solely on phonetic grounds, nevertheless maintained that from a phonological point of view the distinction is essential. The phonetic correlates of the phonological distinctions remained largely speculative in the 1931 paper.

It appears to have been the general standpoint for many European linguists that in word stress both dynamic and musical factors are always present, but that one may predominate. This view appears satisfactory for treating languages in which there are no independent tonal contrasts, i.e., languages in which pitch contrasts are always associated with a stressed syllable. It is not surprising that insistence on the independence of stress and pitch became strong among American linguists who had worked with tone languages in which every syllable could carry contrastive tone, regardless of stress. Among them was Pike (1945), who, studying the well-known minimally contrastive noun-verb pairs in English (of the type PERmit–perMIT), reached the conclusion that intensity carried the distinctive function in such word pairs. The linguists and phoneticians who have criticized the value of intensity as a stress cue (Mol and Uhlenbeck, 1956; Bolinger, 1958; Jassem, 1959) do not seem to have concerned themselves with the question of whether the pitch accents of English or Polish should be treated as tonemes that are analogous to the tonemes of, say, Chinese.

It seems timely to evaluate the evidence regarding the possible independence of fundamental frequency and intensity, on the one hand, and stress and pitch, on the other. Examples were presented earlier of instances in which intensity and fundamental frequency curves go in opposite directions (Serbo-Croatian, Figure 4.3). It is obvious from such instances that there is no automatic positive correlation between increases and decreases of intensity and fundamental frequency. There is evidence that increases in subglottal pressure produce increases in the rate of vibration of the vocal folds; however, one has to assume the possibility of independent control of the vocal fold vibration, since not every peak of subglottal pressure is accompanied by higher fundamental frequency, the converse being also true. Experiments with whispered speech show that in some languages fundamental frequency is distinctive in phonated speech, but distinctions disappear in whispered speech. This suggests that it is the vocal fold adjustment that produces significant fundamental frequency, for if the fundamental frequency were simply a result of differences in subglottal pressure, and consequently a nondistinctive concomitant of intensity, these distinctions should be preserved in whispered speech. I am sure that it is possible to identify a stressed syllable in whispered speech in a nontonal language, although I have not run across a systematic experiment testing this proposition.

These considerations suggest that fundamental frequency and intensity can be considered independent, at least in some cases and to a certain degree. There is solid evidence, however, that various dependence relationships exist between them at the same time. As was mentioned already, increases in subglottal pressure produce an increase in the rate of vibration of the vocal folds, unless there is some compensatory adjustment in their tension. Increases in subglottal pressure also result in greater amplitude of the sound wave, even if fundamental frequency is kept constant (by the just-postulated compensatory adjustment of the vocal folds). This means that each individual pulse produced by the vocal folds contains a greater amount of acoustic energy. Increases in the amplitude of the sound wave normally result in an impression of greater loudness, since a greater amount of energy reaches the ear in a given unit of time. However, from what is known about the integrating time-constant of the ear, it seems that the same effect should be achieved by a greater number of pulses reaching the ear per unit of time. Higher frequency thus should result not only in an impression of higher pitch but also in an impression of greater loudness. At the frequencies of the human vocal range, the ear is also increasingly sensitive to higher frequencies. An increase of perceived loudness can thus be caused both by greater amplitude of the individual pulses (produced by increased subglottal pressure) and by a greater number of these pulses reaching the ear per unit time (as a secondary result of higher subglottal pressure or as a primary result of increased tension of the vocal folds). It is not surprising, then, that the listener may attribute both types of increases to the same underlying cause and call it by a common name, such as stress.

There is no evidence that a listener can distinguish between increases of fundamental frequency that are caused by the two possible physiological mechanisms. However, it is probable that the *speaker* can distinguish between them, since the two mechanisms involve different—and widely separated—organs. The speaker "knows" which syllable he has stressed; the listener uses his knowledge of the language in addition to the phonetic cues present in the sound wave to determine which syllable was stressed. This analysis-by-synthesis approach to stress was anticipated by Daniel Jones (1940), who also discussed the problems involved in identifying the location of stress of unknown languages, and the pitfalls of interpreting prominence achieved by other means as being due to stress (Jones, 1950 [1962]).

Fónagy (1966) reports some results of a study in which Hungarian listeners were asked to identify the stressed syllable in Italian and Rumanian recordings. They misjudged stress in 5.6% of the cases. Fónagy concludes that greater effort can be fairly well reconstructed even if the language is unknown to the listener. Some of the errors were systematic; for example, the listeners identified the first syllable of such words as *passione* and *rapporto* as stressed. The explanation lies in the structure of Hungarian: a stressed syllable can never start with a long consonant in Hungarian, as the stress always falls on the first syllable, and no Hungarian word begins with a long consonant.

It must be concluded that while it is possible to control the physiological mechanisms that underlie the production of stress and pitch independently of each other, there is no evidence available at present to show that speakers do so systematically. It is likewise not proved that the two physiological mechanisms that can be used to produce increases in fundamental frequency are, in fact, used for different linguistic purposes. Third, it has not been shown that a listener is able to distinguish between changes in fundamental frequency brought about by the two different mechanisms. This explains the difficulty in establishing correlations between physical and physiological parameters and perceived stress. Prominence may indeed have several physiological and acoustic components. Intensity and fundamental frequency are probably both factors in the production and identification of a stressed syllable. Languages may differ in the relative importance of one or the other feature, and in the relative independence of the two features.

Other differences between types of stress have been claimed to exist. Jones (1950 [1962]) listed level stress, crescendo stress, diminuendo stress, and crescendo-diminuendo stress. All four have been claimed to exist in Serbo-Croatian (Fry and Kostić, 1939; Trager, 1940). Since later research has confirmed the traditional view that Serbo-Croatian is a tone language, it may well be that these analyses of Serbo-Croatian reflect the kind of interpretation of fundamental frequency in terms of stress that Jones warned against.

I am not familiar with any experimental studies dealing with these kinds of stress differences. Electromyographic studies of the respiratory mechanism and studies of subglottal pressure have brought to light no evidence of differences of this kind. It appears extremely unlikely that intensity can provide a reliable correlate of distinctions like those between crescendo and diminuendo stress; such increases and decreases would have to be distinguished from segmentally conditioned changes in intensity within a syllable nucleus (cf. Section 4.4.1) and from fluctuations in intensity due to interaction between fundamental frequency and formant frequency. The question certainly deserves further study.

4.5.2. Domain of phonemic stress The question concerning the domain of stress can be looked at from two different points of view. According to one, stress itself serves to divide the speech chain into units; stress has an organizing or articulating function. According to the other, the units are determined either by phonetic boundary signals ("junctures") or by morphological-lexical criteria, and the occurrence and distribution of stress is describable in terms of these units. It depends on the size of the units whether we are dealing with word-level stress or sentence stress.

What has to be decided first is the minimum size of the unit of stress placement. From what is known of the activity of intercostal musculature, it appears probable that the smallest unit that may carry stress must be approximately the size of a syllable. The muscular gesture that underlies stress production requires a certain time for its realization, and there are time delays in the system that make it extremely unlikely that stress can be "turned on" to coincide with the duration of a single segmental sound. Even if stress is associated with a mono-syllabic word consisting of a single vowel, phonetically stress is not the property of a single segment. The treatment of any kind of stress as a segmental feature (Lieberman, 1967) thus involves a considerable degree of arbitrariness.

Even though the syllable may be considered to constitute the phonetic domain of stress placement, stressed and unstressed monosyllabic words can only be distinguished within a larger utterance (considering stress here in terms of muscular effort rather than in terms of other factors, such as differences in vowel quality). Thus, the minimal unit of contrastive stress placement is a sequence of two syllables.

If the placement of stress on one of the syllables of the utterance is not predictable by morphological, lexical, or syntactic criteria, stress occupies an independent position within the phonology of the language; the term *phonemic stress*, or *free stress*, is applied to this kind of linguistically significant stress. Languages in which stress functions to distinguish between otherwise identical words include Russian and English. It should be emphasized, however, that languages with unpredictable stress may differ widely with regard to the functional yield of stress. In Yiddish, for example, the distinguishing value of stress within the morpheme is almost nil: there are practically no pairs of morphemes that are distinguished by nothing except the place of stress. On the other hand, the place of stress is very firmly fixed; every Yiddish morpheme that consists of more than one syllable may receive a stress on one of the syllables, but not on others (Weinreich, 1954).

The terms *word-level stress* or *phonemic stress* presuppose that the domain of stress is a word, and that the definition of a word does not depend on a criterion involving stress. There exists another type of stress that serves to combine a sequence of morphemes into a stress construction in which the morphemes stand in a fixed stress relationship to each other. Weinreich (1954) calls this type of stress *constructive stress*. If the constructive stress falls on a morpheme that consists, itself, of more than one syllable, it is rendered on the syllable that has phonemic stress. In English, for example, certain kinds of noun phrases may be turned into compounds by the use of a stress pattern appropriate for compound nouns. It is the stress pattern that turns the sequence of morphemes into a compound; the suprasegmental pattern effectively determines its own domain.

This situation differs from the use of stress as a boundary marker. In a number of languages, the placement of stress on a certain syllable is determined with reference to the word; conversely, the position of stress identifies the word as a phonological unit (Jakobson, 1931). In languages with such *bound stress*, there is no opposition between stressed and unstressed syllables within word-level phonology. Jakobson's examples include Czech, with bound stress on the first syllable of a word; French, with stress on the last syllable; Polish, with stress on the penultimate syllable; and some Macedonian dialects, with stress on the third syllable from the end of the word. Languages with more complicated patterns include Latin, with stress on the penultimate syllable if long, and on the third syllable from the end if the penultimate syllable is short; Old Lesbian, with stress on the penultimate syllable if the last syllable is long, and on the third syllable from the end if the last syllable is short; and Classical Arabic, in which stress falls on the long syllable that is closest to the beginning of the word, and on the first syllable if the word consists only of short syllables.

An intermediate type between phonemic stress and bound stress is *morphological stress* (Jakobson, 1931). In languages with morphological stress, the position of stress is fixed with regard to a given morpheme but not with regard to word boundaries. Morphological stress of this type may differentiate between compound words but not between individual morphemes. This kind of stress distinguishes between the two German verbs *übersétzen*, 'to translate', and *übeʀsetzen*, 'to take across'.

4.5.3. Degrees of stress Another problem to be considered within word-level phonology is the question of degrees of stress. Jones (1950 [1962]) suggests that most stress languages employ two degrees of stress ("strong" and "weak") for effecting distinctions between words. Degrees intermediate between the strongest and weakest stresses are, according to Jones, degrees of prominence due to other phonetic features (such as vowel quality, duration, or pitch) rather than to stress, which Jones defines as respiratory force. Jones observes that in languages like English and German, words are never distinguished by the positions of secondary stresses alone, and that the semantic function of more than two degrees of stress in English appears to be confined to sentences or to compound words of a type that lie beyond the scope of word-level phonology.

It has been widely believed that there are four distinctive degrees of stress in English (Trager and Smith, 1951); however, the phonetic reality behind these four degrees of stress has also been widely questioned. As has been mentioned before, there exists no phonetic evidence for differences in degree of expiratory stress. Chomsky and Halle (1968) submit that the stress contours and other phonetic facts that are recorded by careful impressionistic phoneticians constitute some kind of perceptual reality for those who know the language in question, although there is nothing to suggest that these phonetic observations also describe a physical or acoustic reality. To explain this perceptual fact, they suggest that a person who knows the language "hears" the predicted phonetic shapes; a speaker who utilizes the principle of the transformational cycle and the compound and nuclear stress rules should "hear" the stress contour of the utterance that he perceives and understands, whether or not it is physically present in any detail. Chomsky and Halle proceed to give an elaborate analysis of the stress rules of English without specifying the differences in degrees of stress in phonetic terms.

There is probably a very good reason why these fine gradations in stress cannot be expressed in phonetic terms. It appears probable that word-level stress is in a very real sense an abstract quality: a potential for being stressed. Word-level stress is the capacity of a syllable within a word to receive sentence stress when the word is realized as part of the sentence. The degrees of stress of other syllables within the word are usually predictable by rules and are therefore noncontrastive. This was already brought out clearly by Weinreich (1954), who stated, in his discussion of stress in Yiddish, that stress is not an obligatory loudness at all, but rather a place where relative loudness occurs if the morpheme is to be emphasized in the text. The fact that not all syllables that are perceived as stressed are associated with peaks of subglottal pressure supports the idea that what is realized phonetically is sentence-level stress rather than word-level stress. In other words, our knowledge of the structure of the language informs us which syllables have the potential of being stressed; we "hear" the underlying phonological form.

4.5.4. Sentence-level stress When stress functions at the sentence level, it does not change the meaning of any lexical item, but it increases the relative prominence of one of the lexical items. Bierwisch (1966) distinguishes three kinds of sentence-level stress. Each sentence has, first of all, automatically, a *primary stress* (nonemphatic sentence stress).

Kiparsky (1966) has shown that in German the placement of this primary stress is subject to topicalization rules and therefore is not contrastive. *Contrastive stress* occurs in sequences of sentences with parallel constituents that are filled with different morphemes. In other words, contrastive stress is used to distinguish a particular morpheme from other morphemes that may occur in the same position. *Emphatic stress* is used to distinguish a sentence from its negation. It may occasionally be phonetically indistinguishable from contrastive stress, but there are instances (and languages) in which the two are different. Bierwisch (1966) explains the phonetic difference between contrastive stress and emphasis in German as follows. Both involve the assignment of primary stress to the emphasized constituent (which may differ from the constituent to which primary stress would otherwise be assigned by rules), but emphasis is accompanied by a greater degree of reduction of other stresses in the sentence than is found in the case of contrastive stress. It appears that in Hungarian emphasis affects word order, whereas contrastive stress is manifested by phonological means (Kiefer, 1967).

As was brought out above, there is phonetic evidence that emphasized words are associated with subglottal pressure peaks; emphasis thus has a first-order phonetic correlate which word stress does not seem to have. As is the case with stress in general, emphasis may be reflected in other phonetic parameters than in increased intensity alone. In an extensive acoustic analysis of emphasis in Serbo-Croatian, we established a number of acoustic correlates of emphasis (Ivić and Lehiste, 1969). These consist primarily of a "larger than life" realization of an idealized form of the emphasized word: a wider range of fundamental frequency, increased differences in intensity between the accented and unaccented syllables, increased duration, and a more clearly defined fundamental frequency movement. In yes-no questions, emphasis is manifested by the use of a special type of accentual pattern on the emphasized word, which replaces and neutralizes both the rising and the falling accents (cf. Chapter 3, Section 3.5.4).

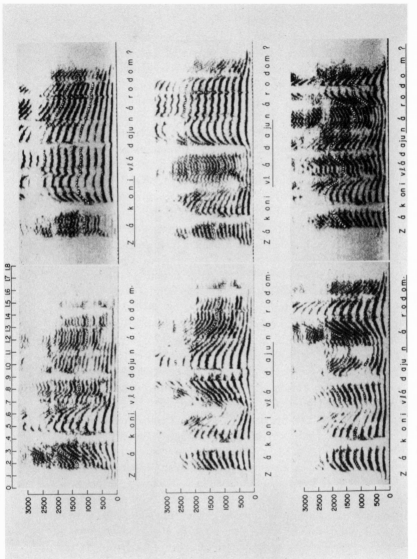

Figure 4.4. Narrow-band spectrograms of six Serbo-Croatian utterances, produced with emphasis on one of the words. Statements are contrasted with yes-no questions (Ivić

Figure 4.4 illustrates the phonetic realization of emphasis in six Serbo-Croatian sentences. On the left side of the figure there are narrow-band spectrograms of the utterance *Zákoni vládaju národom*, 'Laws rule over people', produced as a statement. In each of the three productions, a different word was produced with emphasis. On the right side, the same sentences, with emphasis on the same words, are produced as yes-no questions. All words have the same accentual pattern: they are trisyllabic, with a long rising accent on the first syllable, followed by two short syllables. The nonemphatic realization of this accentual pattern is given in Figure 3.3.

4.5.5. Summary The intensity of speech sounds may be influenced by respiratory effort, by degree of opening of the vocal tract, and by the interaction between fundamental frequency and formant frequency. The perception of stressedness appears to be based on a number of factors, the most influential of which is fundamental frequency. Other phonetic correlates of stress, besides fundamental frequency and intensity, include vowel quality and duration. There is a high degree of interaction between stress and other suprasegmental features.

Stress may function as a boundary signal, in which case its position is fixed within a word-level unit. If the position of stress is unpredictable within the word-level unit, stress functions as an independent variable. The domain of these phonemic stress patterns is at least a disyllabic phonological unit. At sentence level, stress may function as sentence stress, contrastive stress, and emphatic stress.

CHAPTER FIVE
INTEGRATION OF SUPRASEGMENTALS
INTO LINGUISTIC THEORY

In this last chapter, I should like to consider the position of suprasegmentals within linguistic theory. As indicated before, I view suprasegmentals as being intimately connected with phonological units. Suprasegmental features characteristically constitute patterns in time; the domains over which these patterns are manifested are phonological units of varying size (i.e., varying temporal extent). The suprasegmental patterns define the phonological units, and conversely, phonological units are characterized by suprasegmental patterns. The boundaries between the phonological units, on the other hand, are signaled by segmental modifications, which have been treated in linguistic literature under the term *junctural phenomena*. I have dealt with the segmental boundary signals that accompany juncture quite extensively elsewhere and shall not review them here (Lehiste, 1960a, 1962, 1965a).

Thus, the position of suprasegmentals within linguistic theory is, in turn, dependent upon the status of phonological units as such. In the following sections, I shall first summarize the evidence for the existence of such units and then consider the relationships between phonological units and linguistic units established on the basis of other than phonological criteria.

5.1. *Units of performance versus units of competence*

A discussion of phonological units might reasonably start with the question of whether it is possible to establish behavioral (i.e., neuromuscular) correlates of linguistic units, and if so, what is the nature of such units (Fromkin, 1966, 1968; Ladefoged and Fromkin, 1968). The results of many of the studies surveyed earlier answer the first question in the affirmative. Information provided by instrumental phonetics also shows that it is necessary to distinguish between units of performance and units of competence. Ladefoged and

154

Fromkin (1968) argue very persuasively that there is no reason to look for a one-to-one relationship between competence units and performance units. In their discussion of the relationship between competence and performance, they define competence as a set of statements or rules that describe (or, if possible, explain) the language that an ideal speaker-hearer has acquired. The rules do not necessarily explain how actual utterances are produced but only what ideal sentences *can* be produced. A description of how a speaker can say an infinite set of utterances is a specification of their performance. Ladefoged and Fromkin suggest that the construction of an adequate performance model must take into account the important distinctions between the two. A competence model can be a static model; a performance model must be a dynamic model. The neural and muscular systems impose a number of temporal constraints upon performance, both from the aspect of the speaker and from that of the hearer. Many of these constraints have been discussed in the preceding chapters of this monograph.

The size of units that comprise one articulatory program depends at least partially on these constraints. One unit of neural organization seems to be the syllable (Fry, 1964; Kozhevnikov and Chistovich, 1965; Fromkin, 1968). There is strong evidence for this from a number of areas, production as well as perception. Another unit of neural organization in the articulatory program is a sequence of up to seven syllables, called syntagma by Kozhevnikov and Chistovich; this unit corresponds in size to the tone-group of Halliday (1963) and the phonemic clause of Trager and Smith (1951).

There is no question about the rhythmic structure of speech, and it seems reasonable to assume that rhythm is of fundamental importance in the neural organization of performance. Lenneberg (1967) makes a good case for assuming that the rhythmic structure of speech is ultimately related to the relatively constant rhythmic patterns of the electrical activity of the brain, one of which has a frequency of approximately 6 cycles per second. It is surely no accident that this frequency is very close to the frequency with which syllables are produced in speech.

From the point of view of the hearer, i.e., from the processing side, performance is constrained by the limitations of short-term memory as well as by the time it takes for the message to go from the ear to the higher centers of the brain. The "time-constant" of the ear appears to be somewhat shorter than the ordinary duration of a syllable (Miller, 1948), being closer to the duration of a segmental sound.

Very little is known of the neural correlates of units of linguistic competence.

5.2. *Phonological units as units of performance*

I believe that there is a close correlation between units of performance and phonological units, on the one hand, and units of competence and morphological-lexical-syntactic units, on the other hand. A hierarchy of phonological units has been part of the linguistic theories constructed by Pike (1954, 1955, 1960) and Halliday (1961, 1963), although higher-level phonological units have been largely ignored within generative-transformational linguistic theory. Evidence for the independence of phonological units and morphological-lexical-syntactic units comes, in large measure, from the study of suprasegmental patterns. I shall now discuss more thoroughly some instances from my own work that I consider to constitute evidence for the independent existence of phonological units.

The first question to be discussed is the reality of the syllable as a phonological unit. I have claimed for some time that the phonological shape of the words of certain languages, such as Finnish and Estonian, can be described meaningfully and naturally only in terms of syllables. Furthermore, the phonetic realization of certain morphemes in these languages is conditioned by the syllable structure of the word of which the morpheme is to constitute a part. I have treated these questions in some detail in previous publications; the presentation below is a summary, based mostly on several of my earlier papers (Lehiste, 1960b, 1962, 1964a, 1965a, 1965b, 1966).

5.3. Quantity in Estonian

The essential point in the quantity system of Estonian—and one of the chief differences between the Estonian and Finnish systems—is that, in Estonian, quantity cannot be satisfactorily analyzed as something that is associated with segmental phonemes exclusively. In many varieties of Finnish, on the other hand, the quantity of vowels can indeed be viewed as if it were the property of the segments. The opposition between long and short consonants, however, is really an opposition between single and geminate consonants; it can also be viewed as a contrast in the placement of syllable boundaries accompanied by differences in length. A short consonant is opposed to a long consonant only in intervocalic position, which makes the geminate assumption plausible; that the long consonant is a geminate follows also from the fact that a long consonant closes the preceding syllable, which can only be the case if the syllable boundary is located within the consonant. The notion of the openness and closedness of syllables will be discussed later.

In Estonian, the first syllable of a polysyllabic word is in one of three contrastive quantities, which may be called syllabic quantities 1, 2, and 3, or short, long, and overlong. Syllabic quantity is not the sum of the segmental quantities of its components. Several possible consonant and vowel quantity combinations yield the same syllabic quantity; but some combinations that apparently should fall in the same category do not, in fact, produce quantitatively equivalent syllables. For example, a vowel in segmental quantity 1 followed by an intervocalic consonant in quantity 2 yields a first syllable of quantity 2; a vowel in quantity 2 and a consonant in quantity 2 also yield a syllable of quantity 2; a vowel in quantity 1 followed by a consonant in quantity 3, or a vowel in quantity 3 followed by a consonant in quantity 1, yields syllables of quantity 3, although the sum of the segmental quantities is four segmental units in the last two types, as it is also when the vowel and the consonant are both in quantity 2. A syllable that contains at least one sound in quantity 3 is in quantity 3, regardless of the number of other segments and their segmental quantities.

Vowel quantity in Estonian is contrastive only in the first syllable of a word. In a monosyllabic word, the vowel is either long or short, but a short vowel is always followed by a long consonant. In the first syllable of a polysyllabic word, all nine vowels occur in three contrastive quantities, and 19 of the 23 diphthongs occur in two contrastive quantities. Vowel quantity is not independently variable in any other position; the structure of a preceding syllable determines the phonetic length of the vowel of the following syllable. For example, after a short first syllable, the vowel of the second syllable is half-long; its actual duration is approximately between that of vowels in (contrastive) segmental quantities 1 and 2. After an overlong syllable, the vowel of the second syllable is phonetically much shorter. The duration of the vowel of the second syllable varies with the quantity of the first *syllable;* it makes no difference which segmental quantity combination occurs in the first syllable. Thus, the duration of the vowel of the second syllable provides a check on the quantity of the preceding syllable: equivalent noncontrastive vowel durations in the second syllable are preceded by equivalent first syllables. It is obvious, to me at least, that the rules for the phonetic realization of the noncontrastive quantity of the vowel of the second syllable have to be formulated in terms of syllables.

Consonant quantity is not contrastive in initial position. Three segmental consonant quantity contrasts occur between the first and the second syllables, between the third and the fourth syllables, and between the fifth and the sixth syllables, regardless of the structure of the rest of the word. The statement may be generalized to apply to the position between odd- and even-numbered syllables. Of course, the length of words is finite, but there seem to be no nonphonological restrictions upon the number of syllables in a word.

Three-way consonant quantity oppositions also occur between even- and odd-numbered syllables, provided that the preceding syllable is overlong, i.e., contains a combination of vowel and consonant quantities that yields an overlong syllable. If the preceding syllable is either in quantity 1 or in quantity 2, i.e., in short or long (but not overlong) quantity, only two contrastive consonant quantities occur. Of these two quantities, one is clearly phonetically identifiable with consonant quantity 1. The other is ambiguously long and cannot be immediately identified with either quantity 2 or quantity 3 on phonetic grounds. Its phonetic duration is between that of the duration of consonants in quantity 2 and quantity 3 in intervocalic position between the first and second syllable, where three-way contrasts occur.

The distribution of consonant quantity contrasts may be summarized as follows. There are no contrasts in initial position; three contrasts between odd- and even-numbered syllables; three contrasts between even- and odd-numbered syllables if the even-numbered syllable is an overlong syllable; and two contrasts between even- and odd-numbered syllables if the preceding syllable is not overlong. A final syllable ends either in a vowel or in a consonant; in this position, the consonant has two contrastive quantities.

The phonetic realization of consonant quantity thus has to be formulated with reference not only to syllables but to their order number within a word. In order to predict the actual duration of a nonshort consonant, it is necessary to know whether it will occur at the boundary of an even- and odd-numbered syllable or at the boundary of an odd- and even-numbered syllable, and further, whether the preceding even-numbered syllable is overlong or not.

I see no way of accurately predicting the phonetic realization of segmental sounds in Estonian without reference to higher-level phonological units—syllables and sequences of syllables.

5.4. *Morphophonemic alternations in Finnish*

Another way of looking at syllables is in terms of their openness or closedness. An open syllable is, traditionally, a syllable ending in a vowel; a closed syllable ends in a consonant.

The development of a system of morphophonemic alternations in Balto-Finnic languages has long been believed to be connected with the openness and closedness of syllables (Itkonen, 1946). The morphophonemics of Finnish has been subject to considerable attention recently (Harms, 1964; McCawley, 1964; Austerlitz, 1965; Wiik, 1967; Anttila, 1967). This is not the place for a complete review of the different points of view concerning Finnish morphophonemics; I shall just outline briefly my reasons for claiming that the rules for morphophonemic alternation likewise presuppose the existence of syllables. Although the morphophonemic alternations in Estonian are essentially (and historically) the same as in Finnish, I shall use Finnish examples, since the conditioning factors have not disappeared in Finnish to the same extent as they have in Estonian.

In Finnish, many disyllabic morphemes and words have the structure (c)vCv(c), where c stands for consonant, v for vowel, parentheses indicate the possible presence of a consonant, and C indicates a consonant that is subject to alternation. In many words, the quantity of the consonant in intervocalic position between the first and second syllable, denoted with C in the formula, depends for its actual realization on the presence or absence of the following consonant shown in parentheses. The consonant may be part of the morpheme; however, it may also constitute a separate morpheme (a case ending) without any difference in results. If the consonant is present, the so-called weak degree appears; if it is absent, C appears in the strong degree. Thus the morpheme *tyttö*, 'girl', is realized with a long intervocalic -*tt*-, representing the strong degree, in the nominative case; in the genitive, after the suffixation of the genitive ending -*n*, the morpheme appears in the weak degree form *tytön*.

One might now assume that it is simply the presence of the consonant segment, here -*n*, which causes the appearance of the weak degree. This view might be supported by the fact that a morpheme like *tytär*, 'daughter' (nominative singular), likewise has a single -*t*- before the final consonant -*r*. However, this claim cannot be maintained in face of the fact that the genitive singular form of *tytär* is *tyttären*. The *-r-* is still present, but in this instance it is preceded by the strong degree of the intervocalic consonant. The difference between the degrees of *tytär* and *tyttären* is traditionally explained by the Finnish syllabification rule, according to which a single intervocalic consonant starts the next syllable and leaves the preceding syllable open. The difference between the forms with *-t-* and *-tt-* in the morpheme *tytär* is thus explained by the observation that in *tytär* the second syllable is closed, while in *tyttären* the second syllable is open. In other words, the syllable boundary is located before *-r-* in the genitive singular form *tyttären*, while in the nominative singular form *tytär* the second syllable ends in *-r*. Obviously the difference in the placement of a syllable boundary presupposes the presence of syllables.

Let us now consider some of the oblique cases of the words *tyttö* and *tytär*. The adhesive cases of these two words have the forms *tytöllä* and *tyttärellä;* the essive case forms are *tyttönä* and *tyttärenä*. There is a difference in degree between *tytöllä* and *tyttönä*, which can easily be explained by the traditional assumption that in *tyttönä* the syllable boundary is located before *-n-*, while in *tytöllä* the syllable boundary lies within the geminate consonant, so that in *tytöllä* the second syllable is closed (causing the occurrence of the weak degree) and in *tyttönä* the second syllable is open (causing the appearance of the strong degree).

Thus far it might appear that the conditioning is completely phonetic. In that case, however, we should also expect a geminate *-rr-* in the essive case form *tyttärenä*, since the *-r-* here is in analogous position to the *-tt-* in *tyttönä*, occurring before the single *-n-* of the essive case ending. This is clearly not so; obviously not every intervocalic consonant is subject to alternation. In fact the only consonants that undergo degree change occur between the first and second syllables of disyllabic morphemes (leaving aside for the moment the problem of suffixes, some of which are likewise subject to alternation). It is not possible to predict on phonetic grounds which morphemes contain consonants that undergo degree change; Finnish dictionaries (for example, Alanne, 1962) mark those morphemes with an asterisk. The applicability of the rules for morphophonemic alternation thus cannot be formulated solely in phonetic terms.

One might propose a different theory: the degree of a stem consonant depends on the morphological structure of a word, without reference to its syllabic structure. In this case, the strong degrees of the morphemes *tyttö* and *tytär* in the essive case forms *tyttönä* and *tyttärenä* would be conditioned by the presence of the essive suffix. This theory is immediately refuted, however, by the fact that in the (endingless) nominative both strong and weak degree may occur (*tyttö* as well as *tytär*), the same being the case—although with reverse assignment of degree—in the genitive and adessive (*tytön* and *tytöllä* versus *tyttären* and *tyttärellä*).

The rules of morphophonemic alternation are rules for the phonetic realization of morphemes. The type of alternation is a property of a particular disyllabic morpheme and is not phonetically predictable. From the preceding examples, one might have received the impression that only *-tt-* occurs before open syllables, and *-t-* occurs before a closed syllable. The words *tytär* and *tyttö* happen to belong to the class of morphemes whose strong degree is realized with *-tt-* and whose weak degree has a single *-t-*. However, in other morphemes (like *sota*, 'war') it is the strong degree which has *-t-*; in forms in which weak degree is expected, there is a qualitative change. The alternation of *-tt-* with *-t-* is paralleled by an alternation of *-t-* with *-d-*; the genitive singular form of *sota* is *sodan*. This qualitative alternation (and similar alternations in morphemes containing plosives at different points of articulation) is likewise conditioned by the openness or closedness of the following syllable.

The few quoted examples by themselves would prove little; but the principles illustrated by them permeate the whole of Finnish (and Estonian) morphology, the verbal system as well as the nominal one, and although the conditioning factors may have disappeared in individual instances, they can be easily reconstructed. If syllables are not necessary for describing the alternations in the present stage of these languages (which I doubt), they are clearly needed for describing the stage during which these alternations were productive. A satisfactory theory should account for earlier stages of the language as well as for the present stage; and attempts to handle the phenomenon of degree change without reference to syllable structure appear, to me, highly artificial and unnatural.

I believe that the Finnish and Estonian evidence substantiates several claims I have made regarding the independent existence of phonological units, namely, syllables and sequences of syllables. The fact that the rules for the phonetic realization of morphemes must be formulated in terms of phonological units (here, syllables) constitutes additional evidence for the existence of these units. Furthermore, since there seems to be no reason to assume that the nature of the units of competence (here, the morphemes) is in any way affected by these realization rules, the rules also constitute evidence for the existence of units of performance that are in a certain way independent of the units of competence. The interaction between the units of performance and the units of competence is a linguistic fact that can be accounted for when the units of performance are incorporated into linguistic theory. (An interesting first attempt is offered by Fromkin, 1968.)

5.5. Higher-level phonological units

The study of Finnish and Estonian has further brought to the fore the difference between odd- and even-numbered syllables in a sequence. The disyllabic sequence, consisting of an odd- and an even-numbered syllable, appears as a basic phonological building block out of which words seem to be constructed. Indeed, the rules for the occurrence of quantity contrasts in Finnish and Estonian are most economically formulated not just in terms of syllables but in terms of disyllabic sequences (Lehiste, 1965b). The disyllabic sequences are primarily characterized by quantity relationships between the first and second syllable; this becomes especially clear when one studies words consisting entirely of short vowels and consonants, so that segmental quantity contrasts are eliminated (Lehiste, 1965a, 1968a; Lehiste and Wiik, 1968; cf. also Table 4.4).

While monosyllabic words are possible, as are trisyllabic units, most longer words are made up of disyllabic units. In Estonian, quantity patterns characterizing disyllabic units also serve as the form of manifestation when two monosyllabic words are realized as a close-knit sequence. This happens when a compound word consisting of two monosyllabic words loses its bimorphemic nature and begins to function as a noncompound word. In such cases, the word acquires one of the possible quantity patterns of disyllabic words. The same happens when two unstressed monosyllabic words are produced in sequence: instead of two monosyllabic words we find a disyllabic sequence that has the same quantity structure as an equivalent unstressed disyllabic word.

The phonological unit that I have been calling disyllabic sequence has other phonetic characteristics in addition to a quantity relationship between the two syllables. One of these is stress on the first component of the disyllabic sequence. In a Finnish word consisting of a series of disyllabic sequences, the two syllables comprising the sequences tend to have equal intensity, but each successive pair has less intensity than the preceding pair. Thus, an unstressed second syllable may have greater intensity than a stressed third syllable. This already was established experimentally by Sadeniemi (1949), who refers to the disyllabic units as "speech measures," and confirmed by my own studies (Lehiste, 1965a). The disyllabic units also have characteristic fundamental frequency movements.

The relationships between phonological units and lexical units constitute an area in which much further study is needed. I hope to have shown that, in Estonian and Finnish, lexical items are mainly realized in terms of disyllabic sequences. On the other hand, there are several ways in which lexical structure is recoverable within the framework provided by the phonological structure. In Estonian, for example, contrasts in vowel quantity may occur only in the very first disyllabic sequence of a polysyllabic word. Likewise in Estonian, nine vowels may occur in the first syllable of a word (i.e., in a monosyllabic word or the first syllable of the first disyllabic sequence). In all other syllables, only four vowels may occur. Thus, the occurrence of contrastive vowel quantity or the occurrence of one of the vowels that are excluded from nonfirst syllables indicates the presence of the first syllable of a word.

Folksongs provide some additional evidence that users of the language are well aware of the difference between lexical structure and phonological structure. Estonian folk song meter consists of a four-foot trochaic line in which ictus normally falls on a long syllable. Ictus may never fall on a short first syllable of a word, although nonfirst short syllables are tolerated in ictus position. In other words, in a well-formed trochaic line, the boundaries of the feet and word boundaries need not coincide; in fact, a short first syllable of a word *must* fall in the nonictus part of the foot, although words bear lexical stress on their first syllable.

In Finnish, lexical items are further characterized by vowel harmony. The span over which vowel harmony operates is lexically determined, not phonetically conditioned.

Quantity patterns serve to characterize phonological units in a number of other languages, but I should like to review briefly a few instances in which tonal features and stress features have the same function.

Stress seems to have the function of organizing speech into rhythmical units in Czech, a language in which word stress falls predictably on the first syllable and quantity seems to be mainly associated with vocalic segments. Ondráčková (1962) studied the rhythmical structure of a large corpus of Czech utterances. She defined a rhythmical unit as a stressed syllable followed by a number of closely connected syllables. Her material consisted of 64,500 rhythmical units, realized by 95 speakers. Ondráčková found that within a rhythmical unit a word loses its independence. There were some cases in which a longer word consisted of more than one rhythmical unit, and many cases in which a number of words were realized as one rhythmical unit. The only connection between lexically determined words and rhythmical units appeared in the fact that the relatively highest degree of stress, which identifies the beginning of a rhythmical unit, had to fall on the first syllable of a word. The most common sizes of rhythmical units were two syllables (39.5% of the studied units) and three syllables (31%); it depended on the type of material whether one-syllable or four-syllable rhythmical units were next in frequency, but these four types together represented 97% of the material. The longest rhythmical unit consisted of nine syllables; there was just one such occurrence in the material comprising 64,500 rhythmical units.

Several instances have been discussed earlier in which tonal features provide the characteristic patterns whose domains constitute phonological units. It was found that, in Swedish and Norwegian, the minimal domain of contrastive tonal patterns is a disyllabic sequence; however, a pattern may be extended over a word that is longer than two syllables (Elert, 1964), or a pattern may span a sequence of words that stand in a grammatical relationship to one another (Rischel, 1963). Serbo-Croatian provided an example of a language in which features of quantity, tone, and stress combine in an accentual system whose contrastive units are likewise disyllabic sequences. Here, too, a sequence may contain more than one word, as is clearly seen in the treatment of prepositions that form an accentual unit with the following word (Lehiste, 1965a).

There are some ways in which suprasegmental features function within utterances that consist of more than one such word-level or phrase-level unit. Bierwisch (1966) discusses certain instances in German in which phonological factors override the syntactically determined division of an utterance into components. But much remains to be done to establish the nature of phonological units that are greater in extent than the syntagmas of Kozhevnikov and Chistovich, or the rhythmical units of Ondráčková, or the quantity-based "speech measures" of Finnish and Estonian, and to relate these units to syntactic and lexical components of the grammar.

5.6. The quest for phonetic reality

The position of suprasegmentals within linguistic theory thus depends on the more general question of the position of higher-level phonological units within linguistic theory. A detailed comparison of linguistic theories that provide for a hierarchical structure of phonological units with theories that either ignore or deny such a hierarchical structure is beyond the scope of this study. I am convinced, however, that any satisfactory theory must take into account the evidence presented here for the existence of suprasegmental patterns whose domain is larger than a segment.

There are many areas that I would have liked to explore more thoroughly, and many problems that deserve extensive further study. Since my approach has been basically phonetic, I have stopped short of discussing more abstract concepts of prosodic systems. I have given only passing attention to the problems connected with the motor theory of speech perception, partly because a crucial part of the argument deals with segmental sounds, and this book deals with suprasegmentals. I recognize the importance of markedness phenomena in connection with suprasegmentals; but this is largely unexplored ground, and at the moment I would have little to contribute beyond speculation. Sometime in the future, I hope to be able to investigate more fully suprasegmental sandhi effects as well as the role of suprasegmentals in morphophonemic rules. These are some directions further research might take; I hope that this book will provide the groundwork on which a greater theoretical contribution can be built.

Much of the motivation for the work described on the preceding pages has come from a conviction that linguistics is an empirical science. As such, it describes observed linguistic facts, seeks to explain them, and attempts to set up predictions.

The validity of the predictions and explanations depends in a very real way upon the correctness of observations. A comparison of predictions with actual realizations provides the ultimate test of the correctness of the predictions. Phonetic realizations of utterances are the only aspect of language directly subject to observation; and experimental phonetics provides a point at which linguistic theories can be tested with respect to at least one kind of objective reality. The desire for such verification has provided the motivation for the quest for phonetic reality to which this book owes its existence.

BIBLIOGRAPHY

Abramson, A. S. (1961), "Identification and discrimination of phonemic tones," *Journal of the Acoustical Society of America* 33:842 (abstract); Appendix I, Speech Research and Instrumentation, 9th Final Report, 17 Oct. 1960–1 Sept. 1961, Haskins Laboratories, New York.

———— (1962), *The Vowels and Tones of Standard Thai: Acoustical Measurements and Experiments*, Publication 20 of the Indiana University Research Center in Anthropology, Folklore, and Linguistics (Bloomington, Ind.: Indiana University), ix + 146 pp.

Äimä, Frans (1918), "Phonetik und lautlehre des Inarilappischen," *Mémoires de la Société Finno-Ougrienne* 42:1–118, 43:1–249 (Helsinki).

Alanne, V. S. (1962), *Suomalais-englantilainen sanakirja* (Porvoo-Helsinki: Werner Söderström).

Anttila, Raimo (1967), Review of Robert T. Harms, *Finnish structural sketch* (Indiana University publications, Uralic and Altaic Series, Vol. 42, Bloomington, Ind.: Indiana University, 1964). in *Language* 43:566–573.

Ariste, P. (1939), "A quantitative language," in Edgard Blancquaert and Willem Pée (Eds.), *Proceedings of the 3rd International Congress of Phonetic Sciences* (Ghent: Laboratory of Phonetics of the University), pp. 276–280.

Armstrong, L. E., and I. C. Ward (1926), *Handbook of English Intonation* (Leipzig and Berlin: B. G. Teubner).

Austerlitz, Robert (1965), "Zur Statistik und Morphonologie der finnischen Konjugationstypen," *Beiträge zur Sprachwissenschaft, Volkskunde und Literaturforschung* (Steinitz-Festschrift), Veröffentlichungen der Sprachwissenschaftlichen Kommission der Deutschen Akademie der Wissenschaften 5 (Berlin), pp. 39–43.

Avanesov, R. I. (1956), *Fonetika sovremennogo russkogo literaturnogo jazyka* (Moscow: University of Moscow).

Bastian, J., and A. S. Abramson (1962), "Identification and discrimination of phonemic vowel duration," *Journal of the Acoustical Society of America* 34:743–744 (abstract). Paper presented at the 63rd meeting of the Acoustical Society of America, New York, May 24–26, 1962.

————, P. D. Eimas, and A. M. Liberman (1961), "Identification and discrimination of a phonemic contrast induced by silent interval," *Journal of the Acoustical Society of America* 33:842 (abstract).

Benediktsson, H. (1963), "The non-uniqueness of phonemic solutions: quantity and stress in Icelandic," *Phonetica* 10:133–153.

van den Berg, Jw. (1956), "Direct and indirect determination of the mean subglottic pressure," *Folia Phoniatrica* 8:1–24.

van den Berg, Jw. (1957), "Subglottal pressures and vibration of the vocal folds," *Folia Phoniatrica* 9:65–71.

——— (1958), "Myoelastic-aerodynamic theory of voice production," *Journal of Speech and Hearing Research* 1:227–244.

——— (1962), "Modern research in experimental phoniatrics," *Folia Phoniatrica* 14:81–149.

———, J. T. Zantema, and P. Doornenbal, Jr. (1957), "On the air resistance and the Bernoulli effect of the human larynx," *Journal of the Acoustical Society of America* 29:626–631.

Bierwisch, M. (1966), "Regeln für die Intonation deutscher Sätze," *Studia Grammatica* 7:99–201.

Black, J. W. (1949), "Natural frequency, duration, and intensity of vowels in reading," *Journal of Speech and Hearing Disorders* 14:216–221.

Bloomfield, L. (1933), *Language* (New York: Holt).

Bodman, N. C. (1955), *Spoken Amoy Hokkien*, Vol. 1 (Kuala Lumpur).

Bolinger, D. L. (1958), "A theory of pitch accent in English," *Word* 14:109–149.

——— (1964), "Intonation as a universal," *Proceedings of the 9th International Congress of Linguists, Cambridge, Mass., 1962* (The Hague: Mouton & Co.), pp. 833–848.

Boring, E. G. (1940), "The size of the differential limen for pitch," *American Journal of Psychology* 53:450–455.

Borst, J. M., and F. S. Cooper (1957), "Speech research devices based on a channel Vocoder," *Journal of the Acoustical Society of America* 29:777.

Broadbent, D. E., and P. Ladefoged (1959), "Auditory perception of temporal order," *Journal of the Acoustical Society of America* 31:1539.

Catford, J. C. (1964), "Phonation types: The classification of some laryngeal components of speech production," in D. Abercrombie, D. B. Fry, P. A. D. MacCarthy, N. C. Scott, and J. L. M. Trim (Eds.), *In Honour of Daniel Jones* (London: Longmans, Green and Co., Ltd.), pp. 26–37.

Chang, C. T. (1958), "Tones and intonation in the Chengtu dialect," *Phonetica* 2:59–85.

Chao, Y. R. (1930), "A system of tone letters," *Le maître phonétique* 45:24–27.

Chomsky, N., and M. Halle (1961), *The Sound Pattern of English* (New York, Evanston, and London: Harper & Row).

Classe, André (1939), *The Rhythm of English Prose* (Oxford: Blackwell).

Cooper, F. S., A. M. Liberman, and J. M. Borst (1951), "The interconversion of audible and visible patterns as a basis for research in the perception of speech," *Proceedings of the National Academy of Sciences* 37:318–325.

Cowan, M. (1936), "Pitch and intensity characteristics of stage speech," *Archives of Speech Supplement* (Iowa City, Iowa: State University of Iowa).

Craik, Kenneth J. W. (1947–1948), "Theory of the human operator in control systems," *British Journal of Psychology* 38 (1947):56–61; 38 (1948):142–148.

Creelman, C. D. (1962), "Human discrimination of auditory duration," *Journal of the Acoustical Society of America* 34:582–593.

Delattre, Pierre (1962a), "Some factors of vowel duration and their cross-linguistic validity," *Journal of the Acoustical Society of America* 34:1141–1142.

——— (1962b), "A comparative study of declarative intonation in American English and Spanish," *Hispania* 45:233–241.

Denes, P. (1955), "Effect of duration on the perception of voicing," *Journal of the Acoustical Society of America* 27:761–764.

———, and J. Milton-Williams (1962), "Further studies in intonation," *Language and Speech* 5:1–14.

———, and E. N. Pinson (1963), *The Speech Chain*, Bell Telephone Laboratories, Inc. (Baltimore: Waverly Press, Inc.).

Doughty, J. M., and W. R. Garner (1948), "Pitch characteristics of short tones: II. Pitch as a function of tonal duration," *Journal of Experimental Psychology* 38:478–494.

Draper, M. H., P. Ladefoged, and D. Whitteridge (1958), "Respiratory muscles in speech," *Journal of Speech and Hearing Research* 2:16–27.

———, P. Ladefoged, and D. Whitteridge (1960), "Expiratory muscles and airflow during speech," *British Medical Journal* 1:1837–1843.

Durand, M. (1939), "Durée phonétique et durée phonologique," in Edgard Blancquaert and Willem Pée (Eds.), *Proceedings of the 3rd International Congress of Phonetic Sciences* (Ghent: Laboratory of Phonetics of the University), pp. 261–265.

——— (1946), *Voyelles longues et voyelles brèves: Essai sur la nature de la quantité vocalique* (Paris: C. Klincksieck).

Durbin, M., and M. Micklin (1968), "Sociolinguistics: Some methodological contributions from linguistics," *Foundations of Language* 4:319–331.

Efremova, I. B., K. Fintoft, and H. Ormestad (1965), "An experimental study of tonic accents in East Norwegian," *Norsk Tidsskrift for Sprogvidenskap* 20:5–17.

Ekblom, R. (1925), *Quantität und Intonation im zentralen Hochlitauischen* (Uppsala).

Elert, Claes-Christian (1964), *Phonologic studies of quantity in Swedish* (Stockholm-Göteborg-Uppsala: Almqvist & Wiksell).

von Essen, O. (1957), "Überlange Vokale und gedehnte Konsonanten des Hochdeutschen," *Zeitschrift für Phonetik und allgemeine Sprachwissenschaft* 10:239–244.

Faaborg-Andersen, K. (1957), "Electromyographic investigation of intrinsic laryngeal muscles in humans," *Acta Physiologica Scandinavica* 41 (Suppl. 140):1–149.

Fairbanks, G. (1940), "Recent experimental investigations of vocal pitch in speech," *Journal of the Acoustical Society of America* 11:457–466.

———, A. S. House, and E. L. Stevens (1950), "An experimental study in vowel intensities," *Journal of the Acoustical Society of America* 22:457–459.

Falc'hun, F. (1951), *Le système consonantique du breton avec une étude comparative de phonétique expérimentale* (Rennes: Impremeries réunies).

Fant, Gunnar (1958), "Modern instruments and methods for acoustic studies of speech," *Proceedings of the 8th International Congress of Linguists* (Oslo: Oslo University Press), pp. 282–358.

——— (1960), *Acoustic Theory of Speech Production* (The Hague: Mouton & Co.).

——— (1962), "Den akustika fonetikens grunder," *Kungl. Tek. Högskol., Taltransmissionslab. Rappt. No. 7* (2nd printing; Stockholm: Royal Institute of Technology).

Fay, Warren H. (1966), *Temporal Sequence in the Perception of Speech* (The Hague: Mouton & Co.).

Fintoft, Knut (1961), "The duration of some Norwegian speech sounds," *Phonetica* 7:19–39.

Firth, J. R. (1957), "Sounds and prosodies," *Papers in Linguistics 1934–1951* (London, New York, Toronto: Oxford University Press), pp. 121–238. (Originally published in *Transactions of the Philological Society, 1948*).

Fischer-Jørgensen, E. (1954), "Acoustic analysis of stop consonants," *Miscellanea Phonetica* 2:42–59.

——— (1955), "Om vokallaengde i dansk rigsmål," *Nordisk Tidsskrift for Tale og Stemme* 15:33–56.

——— (1959), "Die Bedeutung der funktionellen Sprachbeschreibung für die Phonetik," *Phonetica* 4(Suppl.):7–28.

——— (1964a), "Sound duration and place of articulation," *Zeitschrift für Sprachwissenschaft und Kommunikationsforschung* 17:175–207.

——— (1964b), "Phonometry," *Phonetica* 11:144–154.

Flanagan, J. L. (1957a), "Difference limen for formant amplitude," *Journal of Speech and Hearing Disorders* 22:206–212.

Flanagan, J. L. (1957b), "Estimates of the maximum precision necessary in quantizing certain 'dimensions' of vowel sounds," *Journal of the Acoustical Society of America* 29:533–534.

––––––– (1965), *Speech Analysis, Synthesis, and Perception* (New York: Academic Press).

–––––––, and M. G. Saslow (1958), "Pitch discrimination for synthetic vowels," *Journal of the Acoustical Society of America* 30:435–440.

Fletcher, H. (1934), "Loudness, pitch, and timbre of musical tones,' *Journal of the Acoustical Society of America* 6:59–69.

––––––– (1953), *Speech and Hearing in Communication* (2nd ed.; Princeton, N.J.: D. Van Nostrand Co.).

–––––––, and W. A. Munson (1933), "Loudness, its definition, measurement, and calculation," *Journal of the Acoustical Society of America* 5:82–108.

Fliflet, A. L. (1962), "Einige Beobachtungen über Anschluss und Silbe," *Proceedings of the 4th International Congress of Phonetic Sciences, Helsinki, 1961* (The Hague: Mouton & Co.), pp. 610–615.

Fónagy, Iván (1958), "Elektrophysiologische Beiträge zur Akzentfrage," *Phonetica* 2:12–58.

––––––– (1965), "Zur Gliederung der Satzmelodie," *Proceedings of the 5th International Congress of Phonetic Sciences*, Münster, 1964 (Basel-New York: S. Karger), pp. 281–286.

––––––– (1966), "Electro-physiological and acoustic correlates of stress and stress perception," *Journal of Speech and Hearing Research* 9:231–244.

–––––––, and K. Magdics (1960), "Speed of utterance in phrases of different lengths," *Language and Speech* 4:179–192.

Fourquet, J. (1964), "Zur Deutung der Isophonen der Quantität," *Phonetica* 11:155–163.

Fromkin, Victoria A. (1966), "Neuro-muscular specification of linguistic units," *Language and Speech* 9:170–199.

––––––– (1968), "Speculations on performance models," *Journal of Linguistics* 4:47–68.

–––––––, and P. Ladefoged (1966), "Electromyography in speech research," *Phonetica* 15:219–242.

Fry, D. B. (1955), "Duration and intensity as physical correlates of linguistic stress," *Journal of the Acoustical Society of America* 27:765–768.

––––––– (1958), "Experiments in the perception of stress," *Language and Speech* 1:126–152.

––––––– (1964), "The functions of the syllable," *Zeitschrift für Phonetik, Sprachwissenschaft und Kommunikationsforschung* 17:215–237.

Fry, D. B. (1965), "The dependence of stress judgments on vowel formant structure," *Proceedings of the 5th International Congress of Phonetic Sciences, Münster, 1964* (Basel-New York: S. Karger), pp. 306–311.

―――, and D. Kostić (1939), *A Serbo-Croat Phonetic Reader* (London: University of London Press).

Gårding, E., and A. S. Abramson (1965), "A study of the perception of some American English intonation contours," *Studia Linguistica* 19:61–79.

Garner, W. R. (1951), "The accuracy of counting repeated short tones," *Journal of Experimental Psychology* 41:310–316.

Goldman-Eisler, F. (1954), "On the variability of the speed of talking and its relation to the length of utterances in conversations," *British Journal of Psychology* 45:94–107.

―――― (1956), "The determinants of the rate of speech output and their mutual relations," *Journal of Psychosomatic Research* 1:137–143.

―――― (1961), "The significance of changes in the rate of articulation," *Language and Speech* 4:171–174.

―――― (1967), "Sequential temporal patterns and cognitive processes in speech," *Language and Speech* 10:122–132.

Gray, C. W., and C. M. Wise (1934), *The Bases of Speech* (New York: Harper & Brothers; 3rd ed., New York: Harper & Brothers).

Hadding-Koch, Kerstin (1961), *Acoustico-Phonetic Studies in the Intonation of Southern Swedish, Travaux de l'Institut de Phonétique de Lund* III (Lund: C. W. K. Gleerup).

―――, and A. S. Abramson (1964), "Duration versus spectrum in Swedish vowels: some perceptual experiments," *Studia Linguistica* 18:94–107.

―――, and M. Studdert-Kennedy (1964), "An experimental study of some intonation contours," *Phonetica* 11:175–185.

―――, and M. Studdert-Kennedy (1965), "Intonation contours evaluated by American and Swedish test subjects," *Proceedings of the 5th International Congress of Phonetic Sciences, Münster, 1964* (Basel-New York: S. Karger), pp. 326–331.

Halle, Morris, and K. N. Stevens (1967), "On the mechanism of glottal vibration for vowels and consonants," *Quarterly Progress Report 85*, Research Laboratory of Electronics (Cambridge, Mass.: M.I.T.) pp. 267–270.

Halliday, M. A. K. (1961), "Categories of the theory of grammar," *Word* 17:241–292.

―――― (1963), "The tones of English," *Archivum Linguisticum* 15:1–28.

Hamp, Eric P. (1957), *A Glossary of American Technical Linguistic Usage, 1925–1950* (Utrecht-Antwerp: Spectrum Publishers).

Han, M. S. (1966), *Studies in the Phonology of Asian Languages IV: Vietnamese Vowels* (Los Angeles: Acoustic Phonetics Research Laboratory, University of Southern California).

Hanhardt, A. M., D. H. Obrecht, W. R. Babcock, and J. B. Delack (1965), "A spectrographic investigation of the structural status of *Ueberlaenge* in German vowels," *Language and Speech* 8:214–218.

Hansen, Aage (1943), *Stødet i Dansk*, Det Kgl. Danske Videnskabernes Selskab, Historisk-Filologiske Meddelelser, Bind 29, 1941–1943, Nr. 5 (København: I Kommission hos Ejnar Munksgaard).

Harms, Robert T. (1962), *Estonian Grammar* (Indiana University publications, Uralic and Altaic Series, Vol. 12. Bloomington, Ind.: Indiana University).

—— (1964), *Finnish structural sketch* (Indiana University publications, Uralic and Altaic Series, Vol. 42. Bloomington, Ind.: Indiana University; The Hague: Mouton and Co.).

—— (1968), *Introduction to Phonological Theory* (Englewood Cliffs, N.J.: Prentice-Hall, Inc.).

Harris, J. D. (1952), "Pitch discrimination," *Journal of the Acoustical Society of America* 24:750–755.

Harris, Z. (1944), "Simultaneous components in phonology," *Language* 20:181–205.

Haugen, Einar (1949), "Phoneme or prosodeme," *Language* 25:278–282.

—— (1958), "The phonemics of modern Icelandic," *Language* 34:55–89.

Heffner, R-M. S. (1937), "Notes on the length of vowels," *American Speech* 12:128–134.

Hegedüs, L. (1959), "Beitrag zur Frage der Geminaten," *Zeitschrift für Phonetik und allgemeine Sprachwissenschaft* 12:68–106.

Henderson, A., F. Goldman-Eisler, and A. Skarbek (1966), "Sequential temporal patterns in spontaneous speech," *Language and Speech* 9:207–216.

Henry, F. (1948), "Discrimination of the duration of a sound," *Journal of Experimental Psychology* 38:734–743.

Hill, A. A. (1961), "Suprasegmentals, prosodies, prosodemes," *Language* 37:457–468.

Hint, Mati (1966), "On the phonological transcription of overlength in Standard Estonian," *Soviet Fenno-Ugric Studies* 2:23–36.

Hirsh, I. J. (1959), "Auditory perception of temporal order," *Journal of the Acoustical Society of America* 31:759–767.

Hockett, Charles F. (1955), *A Manual of Phonology*, Memoir No. 11 of International Journal of American Linguistics (Baltimore: Waverly Press, for Indiana University).

Hollien, H. (1960a), "Some laryngeal correlates of vocal pitch," *Journal of Speech and Hearing Research* 3:52–58.

Hollien, H. (1960b), "Vocal pitch variation related to changes in vocal fold length," *Journal of Speech and Hearing Research* 3:150–156.

———— (1962), "Vocal fold thickness and fundamental frequency of phonation," *Journal of Speech and Hearing Research* 5:237–243.

————, and J. F. Curtis (1960), "A laminagraphic study of vocal pitch," *Journal of Speech and Hearing Research* 3:361–371.

————, P. Moore, R. W. Wendahl, and J. F. Michel (1966), "On the nature of vocal fry," *Journal of Speech and Hearing Research* 9:245–247.

————, and R. W. Wendahl (1968), "Perceptual study of vocal fry," *Journal of the Acoustical Society of America* 43:506–509.

Holmes, J. N. (1963), "The effect of simulating natural larynx behaviour on the quality of synthetic speech," *Proceedings of the Speech Communication Seminar, Stockholm, Aug. 29–Sept. 1, 1962* (Stockholm: Speech Transmission Laboratory, Royal Institute of Technology), Volume II, paper F 6.

Hoogshagen, Searle (1959), "Three contrastive vowel lengths in Mixe," *Zeitschrift für Phonetik und allgemeine Sprachwissenschaft* 12:111–115.

House, A. S. (1959), "A note on optimal vocal frequency," *Journal of Speech and Hearing Research* 2:55–60.

———— (1961), "On vowel duration in English," *Journal of the Acoustical Society of America* 33:1174–1178.

————, and Grant Fairbanks (1953), "The influence of consonant environment upon the secondary acoustical characteristics of vowels," *Journal of the Acoustical Society of America* 25:105–113.

Howes, D. H. (1950), "The loudness of multicomponent tones," *American Journal of Psychology* 63:1–30.

Hudgins, C. V., and R. H. Stetson (1937), "Relative speed of articulatory movements," *Archives néerlandaises de Phonétique expérimentale* 13:85–94.

Huggins, A. W. F. (1968), "The perception of timing in natural speech I: compensation within the syllable," *Language and Speech* 11:1–11.

Husson, R. (1960), "Le fonctionnement du larynx comparativement dans la parole et dans le chant," *Acta Linguistica* 10:19–54.

International Phonetic Association (1949), *The principles of the International Phonetic Association* (London: International Phonetic Association; reprinted, 1961).

Isačenko, A. V., and H. J. Schädlich (1966), "Untersuchungen über die deutsche Satzintonation," *Studia Grammatica* 7:7–67.

Itkonen, E. (1946), "Struktur und Entwicklung der ostlappischen Quantitätssysteme," *Mémoires de la Société Finno-Ougrienne* 88 (Helsinki).

Ivić, Pavle, and Ilse Lehiste (1963), "Prilozi ispitivanju fonetske i fonološke prirode akcenata u savremenom srpskohrvatskom književnom jeziku," *Zbornik za filologiju i lingvistiku* 6(Novi Sad): 33–73 (+8 plates).

————, and Ilse Lehiste (1965), "Prilozi ispitivanju fonetske i fonološke prirode akcenata u savremenom srpskohrvatskom jeziku, II," *Zbornik za filologiju i lingvistiku*, 8:75–117 (+11 plates).

————, and Ilse Lehiste (1967), "Prilozi ispitivanju fonetske i fonološke prirode akcenata u savremenom srpskohrvatskom jeziku, III," *Zbornik za filologiju i lingvistiku*, 10:55–93 (+10 plates).

————, and Ilse Lehiste (1969), "Prilozi ispitivanju fonetske i fonološke prirode akcenata u savremenom srpskohrvatskom jeziku IV," *Zbornik za filologiju i lingvistiku*, 12: 115–165 (+10 plates).

Jakobson, R. (1931), "Die Betonung und ihre Rolle in der Wort- und Syntagmaphonologie," *Travaux du Cercle Linguistique de Prague* IV; reprinted in *Selected Writings I* (The Hague: Mouton & Co.), pp. 115–136.

————, C. Gunnar M. Fant, and Morris Halle (1952), "Preliminaries to Speech Analysis, the distinctive features and their correlates," *Technical Report No. 13* (May 1952), Acoustics Laboratory (Cambridge, Mass.: M.I.T.).

Jassem, Wiktor (1959), "The phonology of Polish stress," *Word* 15:252–269.

————, J. Morton, and M. Steffen-Batóg (1968), "The perception of stress in synthetic speech-like stimuli by Polish listeners," *Speech Analysis and Synthesis* 1:289–308 (Warsaw).

Jones, Daniel (1940), *An Outline of English Phonetics* (6th ed.; New York: Dutton).

———— (1948), "Chronemes and Tonemes," *Acta Linguistica* 1:1–10.

———— (1950), *The Phoneme* (Cambridge, England: W. Heffer and Sons, Ltd.; 2nd ed., 1962).

Joos, M. (1948), *Acoustic Phonetics*, Linguistic Society of America Language Monograph No. 23 (Baltimore: Waverly Press, Inc.).

Kiefer, Ferenc (1967), *On Emphasis and Word Order in Hungarian*, Indiana University publications, Uralic and Altaic Series, Vol. 76 (Bloomington, Ind.: Indiana University).

Kingdon, R. (1958), *The Groundwork of English Intonation* (London, New York, and Toronto: Longmans, Green & Co.).

Kinsler, L. E., and A. R. Frey (1950), *Fundamentals of Acoustics* (New York: John Wiley & Sons, Inc.).

Kiparsky, P. (1966), "Über den deutschen Akzent," *Studia Grammatica* 7:69–98.

Kloster-Jensen, M. (1958), "Recognition of word tones in whispered speech," *Word* 14:187–196.

Kozhevnikov, V. A., and L. A. Chistovich (1965), *Speech: Articulation and Perception* (Moscow-Leningrad). Translated by Joint Publications Research Service, Washington, D.C., No. JPRS 30.543.

Kunze, L. H. (1964), "Evaluation of methods of estimating subglottal air pressure," *Journal of Speech and Hearing Research* 7:151–164.

Ladefoged, P. (1960), "The regulation of subglottal pressure," *Folia Phoniatrica* 12:169–175.

―――― (1962a), *Elements of Acoustic Phonetics* (Chicago: University of Chicago Press).

―――― (1962b), "Subglottal activity during speech," *Proceedings of the 4th International Congress of Phonetic Sciences, Helsinki, 1961* (The Hague: Mouton & Co., 1962), pp. 73–91.

―――― (1963), "Some physiological parameters in speech," *Language and Speech* 6:109–119.

―――― (1964a), *A phonetic study of West African languages: An auditory-instrumental survey.* West African Language Monograph Series, No. 1, xix, 74pp., with folding chart and 16 plates. (Cambridge, England: Cambridge University Press [in association with the West African Language Survey]).

―――― (1964b), "Comment on 'Evaluation of methods of estimating sub-glottal air pressure,'" *Journal of Speech and Hearing Research* 7:291–292.

―――― (1967), *Three Areas of Experimental Phonetics* (London: Oxford University Press).

―――― (1968), "Linguistic aspects of respiratory phenomena," *Proceedings of the Conference on Sound Production in Man, Nov. 1966* (New York: New York Academy of Sciences).

――――, M. H. Draper, and D. Whitteridge (1958), "Syllables and Stress," *Miscellanea Phonetica* 3:1–14.

――――, and V. A. Fromkin (1968), "Experiments on competence and performance," *IEEE Transactions on Audio and Electroacoustics*, Volume AU-16, Number 1, pp. 130–136.

――――, and Norris P. McKinney (1963), "Loudness, sound pressure, and subglottal pressure in speech," *Journal of the Acoustical Society of America* 35:454–460.

Lagercrantz, Eliel (1927), "Strukturtypen und Gestaltwechsel im Lappischen," *Mémoires de la Société Finno-Ougrienne* 57 (Helsinki). 1–425.

Lashley, K. S. (1951), "The problem of serial order in behavior," In L. A. Jeffress (Ed.), *Cerebral Mechanisms in Behavior* (New York: John Wiley & Sons), pp. 112–136. Reprinted in S. Saporta (Ed.), *Psycholinguistics: A Book of Readings* (New York: Holt, Rinehart and Winston, 1961), pp. 180–198

Lawrence, W. (1953), "The synthesis of speech from signals which have a low information rate," *Communication Theory* (London: Butterworths Publications), pp. 460–471.

Lehiste, Ilse (1960a), *An Acoustic-Phonetic Study of Internal Open Juncture, Phonetica* 5(Suppl.):1–54.

—— (1960b), "Segmental and syllabic quantity in Estonian," *American Studies in Uralic Linguistics* (Bloomington, Ind.: Indiana University), pp. 21–82.

—— (1961), "Some acoustic correlates of accent in Serbo-Croatian," *Phonetica* 7:114–147.

—— (1962), "Acoustic studies of boundary signals," *Proceedings of the 4th International Congress of Phonetic Sciences, Helsinki, 1961* (The Hague: Mouton & Co.), pp. 178–187.

—— (1964a), "Compounding as a phonological process," *Proceedings of the 9th International Congress of Linguists, Cambridge, Mass., 1962* (The Hague: Mouton & Co.), pp. 331–337.

—— (1964b), *Acoustical Characteristics of Selected English Consonants,* Publication 34 of the Indiana University Research Center in Anthropology, Folklore, and Linguistics (Bloomington, Ind.: Indiana University).

—— (1965a), "Juncture," *Proceedings of the 5th International Congress of Phonetic Sciences, Münster, 1964* (Basel-New York: S. Karger), pp. 172–200.

—— (1965b), "The function of quantity in Finnish and Estonian," *Language* 41:447–456.

—— (1966), *Consonant Quantity and Phonological Units in Estonian,* Indiana University publications, Uralic and Altaic Series, Vol. 65 (Bloomington, Ind.: Indiana University).

—— (1967a), "Suprasegmental features, segmental features, and long components," *Proceedings of the 10th International Congress of Linguistics, Bucharest, 1967* (in press).

—— (1967b), "Diphthongs versus vowel sequences in Estonian," *Proceedings of the 6th International Congress of Phonetic Sciences, Prague, 1967* (in press).

—— (1968a), "Vowel quantity in word and utterance in Estonian," *Congressus secundus internationalis finno-ugristarum, Helsinki, 1965* (Helsinki: Societas Finno-Ugrica), pp. 293–303.

—— (1968b), "Some observations concerning the third tone in Latvian," *Working Papers in Linguistics III* (Columbus, Ohio: Ohio State University, Department of Linguistics) pp. 143–158.

——, and Pavle Ivić (1963), "Accent in Serbo-Croatian: An experimental study," *Michigan Slavic Materials 4* (Ann Arbor: University of Michigan).

Lehiste, Ilse and G. E. Peterson (1959), "Vowel amplitude and phonemic stress in American English," *Journal of the Acoustical Society of America* 31:428–435.

————, and G. E. Peterson (1960), *Studies of Syllable Nuclei 2*, Speech Research Laboratory Report No. 4 (Ann Arbor: The University of Michigan).

————, and G. E. Peterson (1961), "Some basic considerations in the analysis of intonation," *Journal of the Acoustical Society of America* 33:419–425.

Lenneberg, Eric H. (1967), *Biological Foundations of Language* (New York: John Wiley & Sons, Inc.).

Liberman, A. M., F. S. Cooper, K. S. Harris, and P. F. MacNeilage (1963), "Motor theory of speech perception," Stockholm Speech Communication Seminar, Vol. II, Paper D 3 (Stockholm: Speech Transmission Laboratory, Royal Institute of Technology).

————, K. S. Harris, P. Eimas, L. Lisker, and J. Bastian (1961), "An effect of learning on speech perception: The discrimination of durations of silence with and without phonemic significance," *Language and Speech* 4:175–195.

Licklider, J. C. R. (1951), "Basic correlates of the auditory stimulus," in S. S. Stevens (Ed.), *Handbook of Experimental Psychology* (New York: John Wiley & Sons, Inc.), pp. 985–1039.

Lieberman, Philip (1960), "Some acoustic correlates of word stress in American English," *Journal of the Acoustical Society of America* 32:451–453.

———— (1961), "Perturbations in vocal pitch," *Journal of the Acoustical Society of America* 33:597–603.

———— (1967), *Intonation, Perception, and Language*, M.I.T. Research Monograph No. 38 (Cambridge, Mass: The M.I.T. Press).

———— (1968), "Direct comparison of subglottal and esophageal pressure during speech," *Journal of the Acoustical Society of America* 43:1157–1164.

Liiv, G. (1962a), "Udarnye monoftongi estonskogo jazyka," *Akademija Nauk Estonskoj SSR* (Tallinn).

———— (1962b), "On the acoustic composition of Estonian vowels of three degrees of length," *Eesti NSV Teaduste Akadeemia Toimetised*, XI Köide. Ühiskonnateaduste seeria 3, pp. 271–290.

Lindblom, B. (1963), "Spectrographic study of vowel reduction," *Journal of the Acoustical Society of America* 35:1173–1781.

Maack, A. (1949), "Die spezifische Lautdauer deutscher Sonanten," *Zeitschrift für Phonetik* 3:190–232.

———— (1953), "Die Beeinflussung der Sonantendauer durch die Nachbarkonsonanten," *Zeitschrift für Phonetik* 7:104–128.

Magdics, K. (1963), "Researches on intonation during the recent ten years," *Acta linguistica* 13:133–165.

Magdics, K. (1964), "First findings in the comparative study of intonation of Hungarian dialects," *Phonetica* 11:19–38, 101–115.

Malécot, A., and P. Lloyd (1968), "The /t/:/d/ distinction in American alveolar flaps," *Lingua* 19:264–272.

Malmberg, B. (1944), "Die Quantität als phonetisch-phonologischer Begriff," *Lunds Universitets Årsskrift* 41:1–104.

Markel, Norman N. (1965), "The reliability of coding paralanguage: Pitch, loudness, and tempo," *Journal of Verbal Learning and Verbal Behavior* 4:306–308.

McCawley, James D. (1964), Review of Robert T. Harms, *Estonian Grammar* (Indiana University publications, Uralic and Altaic Series, Vol. 12, Bloomington, Ind.: Indiana University, 1962), in *Word* 20:114–126.

Meyer-Eppler, W. (1957), "Realization of prosodic features in whispered speech," *Journal of the Acoustical Society of America* 29:104–106.

Milburn, Braxton (1963), "Differential sensitivity to duration of monaural pure-tone auditory stimuli." Ph.D. Dissertation, University of Oklahoma.

Miller, G. A. (1948), "The perception of short bursts of noise," *Journal of the Acoustical Society of America* 20:160–170.

————, and W. G. Taylor (1948), "The perception of repeated bursts of noise," *Journal of the Acoustical Society of America* 20:171–182.

Miller, J. D. (1961), "Word tone recognition in Vietnamese whispered speech," *Word* 17:11–15.

Mol, H. G., and G. M. Uhlenbeck (1956), "The linguistic relevance of intensity in stress," *Lingua* 5:205–213.

Morton, John, and Wiktor Jassem (1965), "Acoustic correlates of stress," *Language and Speech* 8:159–181.

Must, H. (1959), "Duration of speech sounds in Estonian," *Orbis* 8:213–223.

Nasr, R. T. (1960), "Phonemic length in Lebanese Arabic," *Phonetica* 5:209–211.

Navarro Tomás, T. (1916), "Cantidad de las vocales accentuadas," *Revista de Filología Española* 3:387–408.

Ohala, J., and M. Hirano (1967), "An experimental investigation of pitch change in speech," *Journal of the Acoustical Society of America* 42:1208–1209 (abstract).

Öhman, S. E. G. (1967), "Word and sentence intonation: A quantitative model," Speech Transmission Laboratory, *Quarterly Progress and Status Report* 2–3 (Stockholm: Royal Institute of Technology) pp. 20–54.

Ondráčková, Jana (1962), "Contribution to the question concerning the rhythmical units in Czech," *Phonetica* 8:55–72.

182 BIBLIOGRAPHY

Osser, Harry, and Frederick Peng (1964), "A cross-cultural study of speech rate," *Language and Speech* 7:120–125.

Palmer, H. E. (1922), *English Intonation* (Cambridge, England: W. Heffer & Sons.).

Parmenter, C. E., and S. N. Treviño (1935), "The length of the sounds of a Middle Westerner," *American Speech* 10:129–133.

Peterson, G. E. (1956), "Some curiosities of speech," Paper presented at the 1956 University of Michigan Summer Speech Conference, Ann Arbor, Michigan.

―――, and H. L. Barney (1952), "Control methods used in a study of vowels," *Journal of the Acoustical Society of America* 24:175–184.

―――, and Ilse Lehiste (1960), "Duration of syllable nuclei in English," *Journal of the Acoustical Society of America* 32:693–703.

―――, and N. P. McKinney (1961), "The measurement of speech power," *Phonetica* 7:65–84.

―――, and June E. Shoup (1966), "A physiological theory of phonetics," *Journal of Speech and Hearing Research* 9:5–67.

Pike, Kenneth L. (1945), *The Intonation of American English* (Ann Arbor: University of Michigan Press).

―――(1948) *Tone Languages* (Ann Arbor: University of Michigan Press).

―――(1954, 1955, and 1960), *Language in Relation to a Unified Theory of the Structure of Human Behavior*, Parts I, II, and III (Glendale, Calif.: Summer Institute of Linguistics; 2nd ed., The Hague: Mouton & Co., 1967).

Pipping, H. (1899), "Zur Phonetik der finnischen Sprache," *Mémoires de la Société Finno-Ougrienne* 14 (Helsinki).

Posti, Lauri (1950), "On quantity in Estonian," *Journal de la société Finno-Ougrienne* 54:1–14 (Helsinki).

Raun, Alo (1954), "On quantity in Estonian," *Studia Linguistica* 8:62–76.

Ravila, P. (1962), "Quantity and phonemic analysis," *Proceedings of the 4th International Congress of Phonetic Sciences, Helsinki, 1961* (The Hague: Mouton & Co.), pp. 490–493.

Rehder, P. (1968), "Beiträge zur Erforschung der serbokroatischen Prosodie," *Slavistische Beiträge 31* (München: Verlag Otto Sagner).

Riesz, R. R. (1928), "Differential intensity of the ear for pure tones," *Physical Review* 31:867–875.

Rigault, A. (1962), "Rôle de la fréquence, de l'intensité et de la durée vocaliques dans la perception de l'accent en français," *Proceedings of the 4th International Congress of Phonetic Sciences, Helsinki, 1961* (The Hague: Mouton & Co.), pp. 735–748.

―――(1964), "Reflexions sur le statut phonologique de l'intonation," *Proceedings of the 9th International Congress of Linguists,*

Cambridge, Mass., 1962 (The Hague: Mouton & Co.), pp. 849–858.

Ringgaard, K. (1960), *Vestjysk stød* (Aarhus: Universitetsforlaget i Aarhus).

——— (1962), "The pronunciation of a glottal stop," *Phonetica* 8:203–208.

Rischel, Jørgen (1963), "Morphemic tone and word tone in Eastern Norwegian," *Phonetica* 10:154–164.

Robinson, D. F. (1968), "Some acoustic correlates of tone in Standard Lithuanian," *The Slavic and East European Journal* 12:206–212.

Rosenblith, W. A., and K. N. Stevens (1953), "On the DL for frequency," *Journal of the Acoustical Society of America* 25:980–985.

Rosenzweig, M. R., and W. A. Rosenblith (1950), "Some electro-physical correlates of the perception of successive clicks," *Journal of the Acoustical Society of America* 22:878–880.

Rousselot, P. J. (1924), *Principes de phonétique expérimentale* (Paris: Didier).

Ruhm, Howard B., Eugene O. Mencke, Braxton Milburn, William A. Cooper, Jr., and Darrell E. Rose (1966), "Differential sensitivity to duration of acoustic stimuli," *Journal of Speech and Hearing Research* 9:371–384.

Sadeniemi, M. (1949), *Metriikkamme perusteet* (Helsinki: Suomalaisen Kirjallisuuden Seura).

Saran, Franz (1907), *Deutsche Verslehre* (München: C. H. Beck'sche Verlagsbuchhandlung, Oskar Beck).

Schachter, Paul (1961), "Phonetic similarity in tonemic analysis," *Language* 37:231–238.

Schmitt, Alfred (1924) *Untersuchungen zur allgemeinen Akzentlehre* (Heidelberg: Carl Winter's Universitätsbuchhandlung).

Schouten, J. F. (1940), "The perception of pitch," *Philips Technical Review* 5:286–294.

Sharf, D. J. (1962), "Duration of post-stress intervocalic stops and preceding vowels," *Language and Speech* 5:26–30.

——— (1964), "Vowel duration in whispered and in normal speech," *Language and Speech* 7:89–97.

Shearme, J. N., and J. N. Holmes (1962), "An experimental study of the classification of sounds in continuous speech according to their distribution in the formant 1-formant 2 plane," *Proceedings of the 4th International Congress of Phonetic Sciences*, Helsinki, 1961 (The Hague: Mouton & Co.), pp. 234–240.

Shower, E. G., and R. Biddulph (1931), "Differential pitch sensitivity of the ear," *Journal of the Acoustical Society of America* 3:275–287.

Sievers, Eduard (1893), *Grundzüge der Phonetik* (4th ed.; Leipzig: Breitkopf & Härtel).

Small, A. M., Jr., J. F. Brandt, and P. G. Cox (1962), "Loudness as a function of signal duration," *Journal of the Acoustical Society of America* 34:513–514.

————, and R. A. Campbell (1962), "Temporal differential sensitivity for auditory stimuli," *American Journal of Psychology* 75:401–410.

Smith, Svend (1944), *Bidrag til løsning af Problemer vedrørende Stødet i dansk Rigssprog* (Copenhagen: Kaifers Boghandel).

Snow, W. B. (1936), "Change of pitch with loudness at low frequencies," *Journal of the Acoustical Society of America* 8:14–19.

Stetson, R. H. (1951), *Motor Phonetics* (2nd ed.; Amsterdam: North-Holland Publishing Co.).

Stevens, S. S. (1936), "A scale for the measurement of a psychological magnitude: loudness," *Psychological Review* 43:405–416.

————, and J. Volkmann (1940), "The relation of pitch to frequency: A revised scale," *The American Journal of Psychology* 53:329–353.

Stockwell, R. P. (1960), "The place of intonation in a generative grammar of English," *Language* 36:360–367.

Stott, L. H. (1935), "Time-order errors in the discrimination of short tonal durations," *Journal of Experimental Psychology* 18:741–766.

Straka, G. (1959), "Durée et timbre vocalique," *Zeitschrift für Phonetik und allgemeine Sprachwissenschaft* 12:276–300.

Strenger, F. (1960), "Methods for direct and indirect measurement of the subglottic air pressure in phonation," *Studia Linguistica* 14:98–112.

Swadesh, Morris (1937), "The phonemic interpretation of long consonants," *Language* 13:1–10.

Tarnóczy, T. (1965), "Can the problem of automatic speech recognition be solved by analysis alone?" *Rapports du 5ᵉ Congrés International d'Acoustique*, Volume II, Conférences générales (Liége: D. E. Commins), pp. 371–387.

Tauli, Valter (1966), "On quantity and stress in Estonian," *Acta Linguistica Hafniensia* 9:145–162.

Tiffany, W. R. (1959), "Non-random sources of variation in vowel quality," *Journal of Speech and Hearing Research* 2:305–317.

Timcke, R., H. von Leden, and P. Moore (1959), "Laryngeal vibrations: Measurements of the glottic wave, part 2: Physiological variations," *Archives Otolaryngealogy* 69:438–444.

Trager, G. L. (1940), "Serbo-Croatian accents and quantities," *Language* 16:29–32.

———— (1941), "The theory of accentual systems," in L. Spier, A. I. Hallowell, and S. S. Newman (Eds.), *Language, Culture, and Personality* (Menasha, Wis.: Sapir memorial publication fund), pp. 131–145.

Trager, G. L. (1958), "Paralanguage: A first approximation," *Studies in Linguistics* 13:1–12.

———, and H. L. Smith (1951), *Outline of English Structure*, Studies in Linguistics No. 3 (Norman, Okla.: Battenburg Press).

Trubetzkoy, N. S. (1936), "Die phonologischen Grundlagen der sogenannten 'Quantität' in den verschiedenen Sprachen," *Scritti in onore di Alfredo Trombetti* (Milano), pp. 155–174.

——— (1938), "Quantität als phonologisches Problem," *Actes du IVème Congrès International de Linguistes* (Copenhague), pp. 117–121.

——— (1939), "Grundzüge der Phonologie," *Travaux du cercle linguistique de Prague* 7 (Prague: Cercle linguistique de Prague; 3rd ed., Göttingen: Vandenhoeck und Ruprecht 1962).

Tucker, A. N. (1964), "Kalenjin phonetics," in D. Abercrombie, D. B. Fry, P. A. D. MacCarthy, N. C. Scott, and J. L. M. Trim (Eds.), *In Honour of Daniel Jones* (London: Longmans, Green and Co., Ltd.), pp. 445–470.

Twaddell, W. Freeman (1953), "Stetson's model and the 'suprasegmental phonemes'," *Language* 29:415–453.

Uldall, Elizabeth (1960), "Attitudinal meanings conveyed by intonation contours," *Language and Speech* 3:223–234.

——— (1964), "Dimensions of meaning in intonation," in D. Abercrombie, D. B. Fry, P. A. D. MacCarthy, N. C. Scott, and J. L. M. Trim (Eds.), *In Honour of Daniel Jones* (London: Longmans, Green and Co., Ltd.), pp. 271–279.

Ungeheuer, G. (1962), *Elemente einer akustischen Theorie der Vokalartikulation* (Berlin-Göttingen-Heidelberg: Springer-Verlag).

Vanvik, A. (1963), "Some problems in Scandinavian tonemics,' *Phonetica* 10:165–173.

Wallace, M., and A. I. Rabin (1960), "Temporal experience," *Psychological Bulletin* 57:213–236.

Wallach, H., E. B. Newman, and M. R. Rosenzweig (1949), "The precedence effect in sound localization," *American Journal of Psychology* 62:315–336.

Wang, William S-Y. (1967), "Phonological features of tone," *International Journal of American Linguistics* 33:93–105.

——— (1968a), *The Basis of Speech.* Project on Linguistic Analysis Report 4 (Berkeley: University of California). To be published by Prentice-Hall.

——— (1968b), *The many uses of F_0,* Paper presented at the 1968 Kyoto Speech Communication Symposium. Project on Linguistic Analysis Report 8 (Berkeley: University of California).

Weber, A. O. (1933), "Estimation of time," *Psychological Bulletin* 30:233–252.

Weinreich, Uriel (1954), "Stress and word structure in Yiddish," in Uriel Weinreich (Ed.), *The Field of Yiddish: Studies in Yiddish Language, Folklore and Literature* (New York: Linguistic Circle of New York), pp. 1–27.

Wells, R. S. (1945), "The pitch phonemes of English," *Language* 21:27–39.

—— (1947), "Immediate constituents," *Language* 23:81–117.

Welmers, W. E. (1949), "Tonemics, morphotonemics, and tonal morphemes," *General Linguistics* 4:1–9.

Westin, Kjell, R. G. Buddenhagen, and Dean H. Obrecht (1966), "An experimental analysis of the relative importance of pitch, quantity, and intensity as cues to phonemic distinctions in southern Swedish," *Language and Speech* 9:114–126.

Whorf, L. B. (1946), "The Hopi Language." In Cornelius Osgood (Ed.), *Linguistic Structures of Native America*, Viking Fund Publication in Anthropology 6 (New York: Viking Fund), pp. 159–183.

Wiik, Kalevi (1967), *Suomen kielen morfofonemikkaa*, Publications of the Phonetics Department of the University of Turku, No. 3 (Turku: University of Turku).

——, and Ilse Lehiste (1968), "Vowel quantity in Finnish dissyllabic words," *Congressus secundus internationalis fennougristarum, Helsinki, 1965* (Helsinki: Societas Fenno-Ugrica) pp. 569–574.

Wise, C. M., and L. P-H. Chong (1957), "Intelligibility of whispering in a tone language," *Journal of Speech and Hearing Disorders* 22:335–338.

Wodarz, H. W. (1960), "Über vergleichende satzmelodische Untersuchungen," *Phonetica* 5:75–98.

—— (1962a), "Über syntaktische und expressive Relevanz der Intonation," *Proceedings of the 4th International Congress of Phonetic Sciences, Helsinki, 1961* (The Hague: Mouton & Co.), pp. 800–804.

—— (1962b), "Zur Satzintonation des Polnischen," *Phonetica* 8:128–146.

—— (1963), *Satzphonetik des Westlachischen* (Köln: Böhlau Verlag).

Woodrow, H. (1951), "Time perception," in S. S. Stevens (Ed.), *Handbook of Experimental Psychology* (New York: John Wiley and Sons, Inc.), pp. 1224–1236.

Zimmerman, Samuel A., and Stanley M. Sapon (1958), "Note on vowel duration seen cross-linguistically," *Journal of the Acoustical Society of America* 30:152–153.

Zwirner, E. (1959), "Phonometrische Isophonen der Quantität der deutschen Mundarten," *Phonetica* 4 (Suppl.):93–125.

Zwirner, E (1962), "Beitrag zur Geographie der prosodischen Eigenschaften," *Proceedings of the 4th International Congress of Phonetic Sciences, Helsinki, 1961* (The Hague: Mouton & Co.), pp. 500–518.

————, and K. Zwirner (1936), *Grundfragen der Phonometrie* (Berlin: Metten & Co.; 2nd ed., Basel-New York: S. Karger, 1966).

INDEX

189